BEATÆ VIRGINIS MARIÆ

WITH

THE ENGLISH TRANSLATION.

SUPERIORUM PERMISSU, AC PRIVILEGIO.

Anno Domini 1832.

Cantate Domino cánticum novum: cantate Domino omnis terra.—*Psalmus 95.*

Sing to the Lord a new canticle: let the whole earth chaunt the praises of the Lord.—*Psalm 95.*

DUBLINII:
TYPIS RICARDI GRACE ET FILII,
45, CAPEL-STREET.

Reprint by Veronica Brandt
www.brandt.id.au

ISBN: 978-1-4717-4717-5
Imprint: Lulu.com

OFFICIUM

PARVUM

BEATÆ VIRGINIS MARIÆ.

Pater noster, qui es in cœlis: sanctificétur nomen tuum: advéniat regnum tuum: fiat voluntas tua sicut in cœlo, & in terra. Panem nostrum quotidiánum da nobis hodie: & dimítte nobis debita nostra, sicut & nos dimittimus debitoribus nostris: Et ne nos indúcas in tentatiónem: Sed libera nos a malo. Amen.

Ave, Maria, gratia plena: Dóminus tecum: benedicta tu in muliéribus, & benedictus fructus ventris tui Jesus.— Sancta Maria, Mater Dei, ora pro nobis peccatoribus nunc, & in hora mortis nostræ.— Amen.

Our Father, who art in heaven: hallowed be thy name: thy kingdom come: thy will be done on earth, as it is in heaven. Give us this day our daily bread; and forgive us our trespasses, as we forgive them, who trespass against us. And lead us not into temptation: but deliver us from evil. Amen.

Hail, Mary, full of grace, the Lord is with thee: blessed art thou among women; and blessed is the fruit of thy womb, Jesus.— Holy Mary, mother of God: pray for us sinners, now, and in the hour of death. Amen.

Credo in Deum, Patrem Omnípotentem, Creatorem cœli & terræ. Et in Jesum Christum, Filium ejus unicum, Dominum nostrum : qui conceptus est de Spiritu Sancto, natus ex María Vírgine ; passus sub Pontio Pilato; crucifixus, mortuus & sepultus : descendit ad inferos : tertia die resurrexit à mortuis : ascendit ad cœlos; sedet ad dexteram Dei Patris Omnipotentis : inde venturus est judicare vivos & mortuos. Credo in Spiritum Sanctum, Sanctam Ecclesiam Cathólicam, Sanctorum communiónem; remissiónem peccatorum ; carnis resurrectionem, et vitam æternam. Amen.

I believe in God, the Father Almighty, Creator of heaven and earth. And in Jesus Christ, his only Son our Lord ; who was conceived by the Holy Ghost ; born of the Virgin Mary ; suffered under Pontius Pilate ; was crucified, dead, and buried ; he descended into hell ; the third day he arose again from the dead ; he ascended into heaven ; sitteth at the right hand of God, the Father almighty ; from thence he will come to judge the living and the dead. I believe in the Holy Ghost ; the holy Catholic Church ; the communion of Saints ; the forgiveness of sins ; the resurrection of the body ; and life everlasting. Amen.

A Prayer to be said before the Office.

Aperi, Domine, os nostrum (meum) ad be nedicendum nomen sanctum tuum : munda

Open thou, O Lord, our mouths (my mouth) to bless thy holy name, cleanse our hearts (my

quoque cor nostrum (meum) ab omnibus vanis, pervérsis, et alienis cogitationibus: intellectus (intellectum) illúmina, afféctus (affectum) inflamma; ut digne, attente, ac devotè hoc officium beatæ Virginis Mariæ recitare valeamus (valeam) et exaudiri mereamur (merear) ante conspectum divinæ Majestatis tuæ: Per Christum, Dominum nostrum. Amen.

heart) from all vain, perverse, and distracting thoughts, enlighten our understandings (my understanding), inflame our wills (my will), that we (I) may worthily perform this holy office of the Blessed Virgin Mary, and may deserve to be heard in the presence of thy divine Majesty: Through Christ, our Lord. Amen.

Domine, in unione illíus divinæ intentionis, qua ipse in terris laudes Deo persolvisti, has tibi horas persolvimus (persolvo).

We (I) offer up to thee these hours, and unite our intentions (my intention) with that of Jesus Christ, thy Son, who, while on earth, rendered thee most acceptable homage of divine praises.

A Prayer to be said after the Office.

Sacrosanctæ et indivíduæ Trinitati, Crucifixi Domini nostri Jesu Christi humanitati, beatissimæ et gloriosissimæ, sempèrque Virginis Maríæ fœcundæ integritati,

May all praise, honour, and glory, be rendered by all creatures to the most holy and undivided Trinity, to the sacred humanity of our Lord Jesus Christ,

et omnium Sanctorum universitati, sit sempiterna laus, honor, virtus et gloria ab omni creatura, nobisque remissio omnium peccatorum, per infinita sæcula sæculorum. *R.* Amen.

V. Beata viscera Maríæ Virginis, quæ portavérunt æterni Patris Filium. *R.* Et beata ubera, quæ lactavérunt Christum Dominum.

Pater noster, Ave María, &c.

to the fruitful integrity of the most blessed and glorious Virgin Mary, and to all the saints in general; and may we (I) obtain the remission of all our (my) sins, thro' endless ages. *R.* Amen.

V. Blessed is the womb of the Virgin Mary, which has borne the Son of the eternal Father. *R.* And blessed are the breasts which have nourished Christ, our Lord.

Our Father, &c. Hail Mary, &c.

VESPERS.

O Divine and adorable Lord, Jesus Christ, who hast graciously redeemed us by thy bitter passion and death, we offer up these Vespers to thy honour and glory, and most humbly beseech thee, through thy dolorous agony and bloody sweat, which thou didst suffer in the garden, to grant us true contrition of heart, and sorrow for our sins, with a firm resolution never more to offend thee, but to satisfy thy divine justice for past iniquity.

Ave Maria, &c.

V. Deus, in adjutórium meum inténde. *R.* Dómine, ad adjuvándum me festína.

Glória Patri, et Fílio, et Spirítui Sancto. Si-

Hail Mary, &c.

V. Incline unto my aid, O God. *R.* O Lord, make haste to help me.

Glory be to the Father, and to the Son, and to

cut erat in princípio, et
nunc, et semper, et in
sæcula sæculórum.—
Amen. Alleluia.

the Holy Ghost. As it
was in the beginning, is
now, and ever shall be,
world without end. A-
men, Alleluia.

*From Vespers on Saturday before Septuagesima
Sunday till None on Easter Saturday, instead
of* Alleluia, *is said:*

Laus tibi, Dómine,
Rex æternæ glórie.

Praise be to thee, O
Lord, King of eternal
glory.

*The above is always said at the beginning of
every canonical hour: but Matins and Complin
begin by another Versicle.*

(*Per annum*) Anti-
phona. Dum esset rex.

(*Through the year*)
Anthem. While the
king was.

(*In Adventu*) Anti-
phona. Missus est Ga-
briel angelus.

(*In Advent*) Anthem.
The angel Gabriel was
sent.

(*Tempore Nativ.*)
Antiphona. O admirá-
bile commércium!

(*Christmas time*) An-
them. O admirable in-
tercourse!

Psalmus cix.

Psalm 109.

Dixit Dóminus Dó-
mino meo:* Sede à dex-
tris meis,

The Lord said to my
Lord:* Sit thou on my
right hand,

Donec ponam inimí-
cos tuos,* scabéllum pe-
dum tuórum.

Until I make thy
enemies * thy footstool.

Virgam virtútis tuæ
emíttet Dóminus ex

The Lord shall send
forth the sceptre of thy

Sion :* domináre in médio inimicórum tuórum.

Tecum princípium in die virtútis tuæ, in splendóribus sanctórum :* ex útero ante lucíferum génui te.

Jurávit Dóminus, et non pœnitébit eum : Tu es Sacérdos in ætérnum, secúndum órdinem Melchísedech.

Dóminus a dextris tuis :* confrégit in die iræ suæ reges.

Judicábit in natiónibus, implébit ruínas :* conquassábit cápita in terra multórum.

De torrénte in via bibet :* proptéreà exaltábit caput.

℣ Glória Patri, et Filio,* et Spirítui Santo :

Sicut erat in princípio, et nunc, et semper,*

power out of Sion :* rule thou in the midst of thy enemies.

Thine shall be sovereignty in the day of thy might, in the brightness of the saints :* from the womb before the day-star I begot thee.

The Lord hath sworn, and he will not repent :* Thou art a priest for ever, according to the order of Melchisedech.

The Lord on thy right hand, * has subdued kings in the day of his wrath.

He shall judge the nations, he shall fill ruins :* he shall crush heads in the land of many.

Of the brook he shall drink in the way :* therefore shall he raise up his head.

Glory be to the Father, and to the Son,* and to the Holy Ghost :

As it was in the beginning, is now, and

et in sæcula sæculórum. Amen.

ever shall be, * world without end. Amen.

This Glory be to the Father, &c. *is said at the end of every Psalm.*

(*Per annum*) *Antiphona.* Dum esset Rex in accúbitu suo, nardus mea dedit odórem suavitátis.

(*Through the year*) *Anthem.* Whilst the King was on his couch, my perfumes sent forth an odour of sweetness.

Antiph. Læva ejus.

Anth. His left hand.

(*In Adventu.*) *Antiphona.* Missus est Gábriel ángelus ad Maríam Vírginem desponsátam Joseph.

(*In Advent*) *Anthem.* The angel Gabriel was sent to the Virgin Mary, espoused to Joseph.

Antiph. Ave, María.

Anth. Hail, Mary.

(*Tempore Nativ.*) *Antiphona.* O admirábile commércium! Creátor géneris humáni, animatum corpus sumens, de Vírgine nasci dignátus est; et procédens homo sine sémine, largítus est nobis suam Deitátem.

(*Christmas time*) *Anthem.* O wonderful intercourse! the Creator of mankind, assuming a body animated with a soul, was pleased to be born of a Virgin; and becoming man without human concurrence, he made us partakers of his divine nature.

Antiph. Quando natus es.

Anth. When thou wast born.

Psalmus cxii.

Psalm 112.

LAUDATE púeri, Dó-

PRAISE the Lord, ye

minum : * laudáte nomen Dómini.

Sit nomen Dómini benedictum, * ex hoc nunc, et usque in sæculum.

A solis ortu usque ad occásum, * laudábile nomen Dómini.

Excélsus super omnes gentes Dóminus : * et super cœlos glória ejus.

Quis sicut Dóminus Deus noster, qui in altis hábitat, * et humília réspicit in cœlo et in terra?

Súscitans a terra ínopem, * et de stércore érigens páuperem.

Ut cóllocet eum cum princípibus, * cum principibus pópuli sui.

Qui habitáre facit stérilem in domo, * matrem filiórum lætántem.

servants of the Lord : * praise ye the name of the Lord.

Let the name of the Lord be blessed, * now and for evermore.

From the rising of the sun to the setting thereof, * worthy of praise is the name of the Lord.

High is the Lord above all nations : * and above the heavens in his glory.

Who is like unto the Lord our God, who dwelleth on high, * and regardeth what is humble in heaven and on earth?

Raising up the needy one from the earth, * and from the dunghill lifting up the poor one.

To place him with the princes, * with the princes of his people.

Who maketh the barren woman to dwell in her house, * the joyful mother of many children.

Glória Patri, &c.

(*Per annum*) *Antiphona*. Læva ejus sub cápite meo: et déxtera illius amplexábitur me.

Antiph. Nigra sum, sed formósa.

(*In Adventu*) *Antiphona*. Ave, María, grátia plena, Dóminus tecum: benedícta tu in muliéribus.

Antiph. Ne timeas, María.

(*Tempore Nativ.*) *Antiphona*. Quando natus es ineffabíliter ex Vírgine, tunc implétæ sunt Scripturæ: sicut plúvia in vellus descendísti, ut salvum fáceres genus humánum: te laudámus, Deus noster.

Antiph. Rubum quem viderat Moyses.

Psalmus cxxi.

Lætatus sum in his, quæ dicta sunt mihi: * in domum Dómini íbimus.

Glory be to the Father, &c.

(*Through the year*) *Anthem*. His left hand is under my head: and his right shall embrace me.

Anth. I am black, but beautiful.

(*In Advent*) *Anthem*. Hail, Mary, full of grace, the Lord is with thee: blessed art thou among women.

Anth. Do not fear, Mary.

(*Christmas time*) *Anthem*. When thou wast born after an ineffable manner, the Scriptures then were fulfilled: thou didst descend like rain upon a fleece to save mankind: O our God, we give thee praise.

Anth. The bush, which Moses saw.

Psalm 121.

I rejoiced in what hath been told me: * We are to go up to the house of the Lord.

Stantes erant pedes nostri* in átriis tuis, Jerúsalem.

Jerúsalem, quæ ædificàtur ut cívitas, * cujus participátio ejus in idípsum.

Illuc enim ascendérunt tribus, tribus Dómini;* testimónium Israel ad confiténdum nómini Dómini.

Quia illic sedérunt sedes in judicio,* sedes super domum David.

Rogáte quæ ad pacem sunt Jerúsalem: * et abundántia diligéntibus te.

Fiat pax in virtúte tua;* et abundántia in túrribus tuis.

Propter fratres meos et próximos meos, * loquébar pacem de te.

Propter domum Dómini, Dei nostri,* quæsívi bona tibi.

Glória Patri, &c.

Our feet have stood * in thy courts, O Jerusalem.

Jerusalem, which is now building like a city, * all whose parts are joined together.

For thither the tribes went up, the tribes of the Lord; * according to the ordinances given to Israel to praise the name of the Lord.

For there were placed the judgment-seats, * the judgment-seats over the house of David.

Ask for what tends to the peace of Jerusalem : * and may plenty be to all, who love thee.

May peace be in thy strength; * and plenty within thy walls.

For the sake of my brethren and of my neighbours, * I have advocated thy peace.

For the sake of the house of the Lord, our God, * I have sought good things for thee.

Glory be to the Father, &c.

(Per annum) Antiphona. Nigra sum, sed formósa, filiæ Jerúsalem: ídeo diléxit me rex et introduxit me in cubículum suum.

Antiph. Jam hiems trànsiit.

(In Adventu) Antiphona. Ne tímeas, María; invenisti grátiam apud Dóminum: ecce concìpies, et páries Fílium.

Antiph. Dabit ei Dóminus.

(Tempore Nativ.) Antiphona. Rubum, quem víderat Móyses incombústum, conservatam agnóvimus tuam laudàbilem virginitàtem: Dei génitrix, intercéde pro nobis.

Antiph. Germinávit radix Jesse.

Psalmus cxxvi.

Nisi Dóminus ædificaverit domum,* in va-

(Through the year) Anthem. I am black, but beautiful, O ye daughters of Jerusalem: therefore hath the king loved me, and brought me into his chamber.

Anth. The winter is now past.

(In Advent) Anthem. Do not fear, Mary; thou hast found grace with the Lord: behold thou shalt conceive, and bring forth a Son.

Anth. The Lord will give.

(Christmas time) Anthem. In the bush, which Moses saw burn without consuming, we acknowledge the preservation of thy glorious virginity: O mother of God, make intercession for us.

Anth. The root of Jesse hath budded forth.

Psalm 126.

Unless the Lord himself shall build up

num laboravérunt, qui ædíficant eam.

Nisi Dóminus custodíerit civitátem,* frustra vígilat, qui custódit eam.

Vanum est vobis ante lucem sùrgere :* sùrgite post quam sedéritis, qui manducátis panem dolóris.

Cum déderit deléctis suis somnum : * ecce, hæréditas Dómini, fílii, merces fructus ventris.

Sicut sagíttæ in manu poténtis,* ita fílii excussórum.

Beátus vir, qui implévit desidérium suum ex ipsis;* non confundétur cum loquétur inimícis suis in porta.

Glória Patri, &c.

(*Per annum*) Anti-

the house, * in vain have laboured the builders thereof.

Unless the Lord shall guard the city, * in vain watcheth the sentinel thereof.

It is in vain for you to rise before the light: * arise after you have taken rest, you who eat the bread of sorrow.

Since he will give sleep to his beloved ones : * behold, children are an inheritance from the Lord, the fruit of the womb is a reward.

Like arrows in the hand of a man of power, * so shall be the children of those, who have been rejected.

Blessed is the man, whose desire is filled with them; * he shall not be confounded, when he shall speak to his enemies at the gate.

Glory be to the Father.

(*Through the year*)

phona. Jam hiems tránsiit: imber àbiit et recéssit: surge, amíca mea, et veni.

Antiph. Speciósa facta es.

(*In Adventu*) *Antiphona.* Dabit ei Dóminus sedem David, patris ejus, et regnàbit in ætérnum.

Anth. Ecce ancílla Dómini.

(*Tempore Nativ.*) *Antiphona.* Germinàvit radix Jesse: orta est stella ex Jacob: virgo péperit Salvatórem: te laudàmus, Deus noster.

Anth. Ecce, María génuit.

Psalmus cxlvii.

LAUDA Jerúsalem Dóminum: * lauda Deum tuum Sion.

Quóniam comfortávit seras portárum tuárum: * benedíxit fíliis tuis in te.

Anthem. Now the winter is past, the rain is over and gone: arise, my love, and come.

Anthem. Thou art become beautiful.

(*In Advent*) *Anthem.* The Lord will give him the throne of David, his father, and he shall reign for ever.

Anth. Behold the handmaid of the Lord.

(*Christmas time*) *Anthem.* The root of Jesse hath budded forth: a star hath arisen out of Jacob: a Virgin hath brought forth the Saviour: we give thee praise, O our God.

Anth. Behold, Mary hath borne.

Psalm 147.

O JERUSALEM, praise the Lord: * praise thy God, O Sion.

For strong hath he made the bolts of thy gates: * he hath blessed thy children within thy walls.

Qui pósuit fines tuos pacem :* et ádipe fruménti satiát te.

It is he, who hath settled peace within thy borders : * with the finest flour of wheat he feedeth thee.

Qui emíttit elóquium suum terræ : * velóciter currit sermo ejus.

'Tis he, who sendeth forth his orders to the earth : * his orders go with speed.

Qui dat nivem sicut lanam : * nébulam sicut cínerem spargit.

'Tis he, who sendeth snow like flocks of wool : * he sprinkleth his hoar-frost like ashes.

Mittit crystállum suam sicut buccéllas : * ante fáciem frígoris ejus quis sustinébit ?

He sendeth down his hail like mouthfuls : * who can stand the cold thereof ?

Emíttet verbum suum, et liquefáciet ea ;* flabit spíritus ejus, et fluent aquæ.

He will send forth his word, which shall melt it away : * his spirit shall breathe, and the waters shall flow again.

Qui annúntiat verbum suum Jacob : * justitias et judícia sua Israel.

'Tis he, who maketh known his commandments to Jacob : * his law and ordinances to Israel.

Non fecit táliter omni natiòni :* et judícia sua non manifestávit eis.

He hath not done thus to every nation : * nor hath he made known his law to them.

Glória Patri, &c.

Glory be to the Father.

(*Per annum*) *Antiphona*. Speciósa facta es, suavis in delíciis tuis, sancta Dei génitrix.

(*Through the year*) *Anthem*. Thou art become beautiful and sweet in thy delights, O holy Mother of God.

(*In Adventu*) *Antiphona*. Ecce ancílla Dómini, fiat mihi secúndùm verbum tuum.

(*In Advent*) *Anthem*. Behold the handmaid of the Lord: be it done to me according to thy word.

(*Tempore Nativ.*) *Antiphona*. Ecce, María génuit nobis Salvatórem, quem Joánnes videns exclamávit, dicens: Ecce, Agnus Dei, ecce, qui tollit peccáta mundi, allelùia.

(*Christmas time*) *Anthem*. Behold, Mary hath borne us the Saviour, whom John seeing, exclaimed: Behold the Lamb of God, behold him, who taketh away the sins of the world, alleluia.

(*Through the year, except in Advent.*)

Capitulum. Eccl. xxiv.

Little Chapter, Ec. 24.

AB inítio, et ante sæcula creáta sum, et usque ad futúrum sæculum non désinam: et in habitatióne sancta coram ipso ministrávi. *R.* Deo grátias.

FROM the beginning, and before all ages was I created, and I shall not cease to be in the world to come; and I have ministered before him in his holy abode. *R.* Thanks be to God.

(*In Advent.*)

Capitulum. Isaiæ xi.

Little Chapter. Isa. 11.

EGREDIETUR virga de

THERE shall come

radíce Jesse, et flos de radíce ejus ascéndet: et requiéscet super eum Spíritus Dómini. *R.* Deo grátias.

forth a rod out of the root of Jesse, and a flower shall spring out of its root: and the Spirit of the Lord shall rest upon him. *R.* Thanks be to God.

At the first strophe (or four verses) of the following Hymn they all kneel down.

Hymnus.	*Hymn.*
Ave, maris stella	Bright Mother of our Maker, hail,
Dei mater alma,	Thou virgin ever blest;
Atque semper virgo,	The ocean's Star, by which we sail,
Felix cœli porta.	And gain the port of rest.
Sumens illud Ave	While we this Hail address'd to thee
Gabriélis ore,	From Gabriel's mouth rehearse,
Funda nos in pace,	Obtain that peace our lot may be,
Mutans Hevæ nomen.	And Eva's name reverse.
Solve vincla reis,	Release our long-entangled mind
Profer lumen cæcis,	From all the snares of ill;
Malla nostra pelle,	With heav'nly light instruct the blind,
Bona cuncta posce.	And all our vows fulfil.
Monstra te esse matrem,	Exert for us a mother's care,

Sumat per te preces,	And us thy children own,
Qui pro nobis natus,	Prevail with him to hear our pray'r,
Tulit esse tuus.	Who chose to be thy Son.
Virgo singuláris,	O spotless maid, whose virtues shine,
Inter omnes mitis,	From all suspicion free;
Nos culpis solútos.	Each action of our lives refine,
Mites fac et castos,	And make us pure like thee.
Vitam præsta puram,	Preserve our lives unstain'd with ill
Iter para tutum,	In this infectious way,
Ut vidéntes Jesum,	That heav'n alone our souls may fill
Semper collætémur.	With joys, that ne'er decay.
Sit laus Deo Patri,	To God the Father endless praise;
Summo Christo decus,	To God the Son the same,
Spirítui Sancto,	And Holy Ghost, whose equal rays
Tribus honor unus.— Amen.	One equal glory claim. Amen.
V. Diffúsa est gratia in lábiis tuis. *R.* Proptéreà benedíxit te Deus in ætérnum.	*V.* Grace is spread on thy lips. *R.* Therefore God hath blessed thee for ever.
(*Per annum*) *Antiphona.* Beáta mater.	(*Through the year*) *Anthem.* O blessed mother.

(*Tempore paschali*)
Antiph. Regína cœli.
(*In Adventu*) *Antiph.*
Spíritus Sanctus.
(*Tempore Nativ.*) *Antiph.* Magnum hæreditátis mysterium.

Canticum beatæ Mariæ Virginis. Lucæ i. xlvi.

Magnificat * ánima mea Dominum.

Et exultávit spíritus meus * in Deo salutári meo.

Quia respéxit humilitátem ancíllæ suæ : * ecce enim ex hoc beátam me dicent omnes generatiónes.

Quia fecit mihi magna qui potens es ; * sanctum nomen ejus.

Et misericórdia ejus à progénie in progénies * timéntibus eum.

Fecit poténtiam in bráchio suo : * dispérsit supérbos mente cordis sui.

Depósuit poténtes de

(*Easter time*) *Anth.*
O Queen of heaven.
(*In Advent.*) *Anth.*
The Holy Ghost.
(*Christmas time*) *An.*
Great is the mystery of our inheritance.

Canticle of the blessed Virgin Mary. Luke 1. 46.

My soul doth magnify * the Lord.

And my spirit hath rejoiced * in God my Saviour.

Because he hath regarded the humility of his handmaid : * behold from henceforth all generations shall call me blessed.

For he, who is mighty, hath done great things to me ; * and holy is his name.

And his mercy is from generation to generation * to them who fear him.

He hath shewn might in his arm : * he hath scattered the proud in the conceit of their heart.

He hath cast down

sede, * et exaltávit húmiles.

Esuriéntes implévit bonis, * et dívites dimísit ináues.

Suscépit Israel púerum suum, * recordátus misericórdiæ suæ.

Sicut locútus est ad patres nostros; * Abraham, et sémini ejus in sæcula.

Glória Patri, &c.

(*Per annum*) *Antiphona.* Beáta mater, et intácta virgo, gloriósa regína mundi, intercéde pro nobis ad Dominum.

(*Tempore Paschali*) *Antiphona.* Regína cœli lætáre, allelúia, quia quem meruísti portáre, allelúia, resurréxit sicut dixit, allelúia : ora pro nobis Deum, allelúia.

(*In Adventu*) *Antiphona.* Spíritus Sanctus in te descéndet, Ma-

the mighty from their seat, * and hath exalted the humble.

He hath filled the hungry with good things, * and the rich he hath sent away empty.

He hath received Israel his servant, * being mindful of his mercy.

As he spoke to our Fathers; * to Abraham, and to his seed for ever.

Glory be to the Father.

(*Through the year*) *Anthem.* O blessed mother, and chaste virgin, glorious queen of the world, make intercession for us to the Lord.

(*Easter time*) *Anth.* O Queen of heaven rejoice, alleluia, because he whom thou didst deserve to bear, alleluia, is risen again, as he foretold, alleluia: pray for us to God, alleluia.

(*In Advent*) *Anthem.* The Holy Ghost shall come upon thee, Mary;

ria : ne tímeas, habebis in útero fílium Dei, allelúia.

(*Tempore Nativ.*) *Antiphona.* Magnum hæreditátis mystérium : templum Dei factus est úterus nesciéntis virum : non est pollútus ex ea carnem assumens : omnes gentes vénient dicéntes : Glória tibi, Dómine.

Kyrie eleíson. Christe eleíson. Kyrie eleíson.

V. Dómine exáudi oratiónem meam. *R.* Et clamor meus ad te véniat.

do not fear, thou shalt have in thy womb the Son of God, alleluia.

(*Christmas time*) *Anthem.* Great is the mystery of our inheritance ; the womb of a pure virgin became the temple of God : he, who took flesh of her, was not defiled : all nations shall come and say : Glory be to thee, O Lord.

Lord, have mercy on us, Christ, have mercy on us. Lord, have mercy on us.

V. O Lord, hear my prayer. *R.* And let my cry come unto thee.

If the president be a priest or deacon, instead of the last Versicle is always said the following ; observe this at each hour before and after the prayer :—

V. Dóminus vobiscum. *R.* Et cum Spíritu tuo.

Oremus.

(*Per annum*) Concede nos fámulos tuos, quæsumus, Dómine

V. The Lord be with you. *R.* And with thy Spirit.

Let us pray.

(*Through the year*) Grant, we beseech thee, O Lord God, that

VESPERS.

Deus, perpétua mentis, et córporis sanitáte gaudére; et, gloriósa beátæ Maríæ semper Vírginis intercessióne, a præsénti liberári tristítia, et ætérna pérfrui lætítia. Per Christum Dominum nostrum. R. Amen.

Oremus.
(*In Adventu*) DEUS, qui de beátæ Maríæ vírginis útero, Verbum tuum, Angelo nuntiánte, carnem suscípere voluísti; præsta supplícibus tuis, ut, qui vere eam genitrícem Dei crédimus, ejus apud te intercessiónibus adjuvémur. Per eundem Christum, Dóminum nostrum. R. Amen.

Oremus.
(*Tempore Nativ.*)— DEUS, qui salútis ætérnæ beátæ Maríæ virginitáte fœcúnda, humáno géneri præmia præsti-

we, thy servants, may enjoy constant health of mind and body: and by the glorious intercession of the ever blessed Virgin Mary, may be delivered from all temporal afflictions, and enjoy eternal bliss. Through Christ, our Lord. R. Amen.

Let us pray.
(*In Advent*) O GOD, who was pleased that thy eternal word, when the angel delivered his message, should take flesh in the womb of the blessed Virgin Mary; give ear to our humble petitions, and grant that we, who believe her to be truly the mother of God, may be assisted by her prayers. Through the same Christ, our Lord. R. Amen.

Let us pray.
(*Christmas time*) O GOD, who by the fruitful virginity of blessed Mary, hast given to mankind the rewards of

tísti; tríbue, quæsumus, ut ipsam pro nobis intercédere sentiámus, per quam merúimus auctórem vitæ suscípere Dóminum nostrum, Jesum Christum, Filium tuum. *R*. Amen.

eternal salvation; grant, we beseech thee, that we may experience her intercession, by whom we have received the author of life, our Lord, Jesus Christ, thy Son. *R*. Amen.

Commemoration for the Saints.
(*Through the year, except in Advent.*)

Antiphona. Sancti Dei omnes intercédere dignémini pro nostra omniúmque salúte.

Anthem. All ye saints of God, vouchsafe to make intercession for the salvation of us, and of all mankind.

V. Lætámini in Dómino, exultáte, justi. *R.* Et gloriámini, omnes recti corde.

V. Rejoice in the Lord, ye just, and be exceedingly glad. *R.* And exult in glory, all ye upright of heart.

Oremus.

Protege, Dómine, pópulum tuum, et Apostolórum tuórum Petri et Pauli, et aliórum Apostolórum patrócinio confidéntem, perpétua defensióne consérva.

Let us pray.

Protect, O Lord, thy people, and grant us thy continual assistance, which we humbly beg with confidence, through the intercession of St. Peter and St. Paul, and of thy other apostles.

Omnes Sancti tui, quæsumus Dómine, nos

May all thy Saints, we beseech thee, O Lord,

ubíque àdjuvent; ut dum eórum mérita recólimus, patrocínia sentiámus: et pacem tuam nostris concéde tempóribus, et ab Ecclésia tua cunctam repélle nequítiam: iter, actus, et voluntátes nostras, et ómnium famulórum tuórum, in salútis tuæ prosperitáte dispóne: benefactóribus nostris sempitérna bona retríbue, et ómnibus fidélibus defúnctis réquiem æternam concéde. Per Dóminum, nostrum Jesum Christum, Fílium tuum, qui tecum vivit et regnat in unitáte Spíritus Sancti Deus, per ómnia sæcula sæculórum. *R.* Amen.

always assist our weakness, that whilst we celebrate their merits, we may experience their protection; grant us thy peace in our days, and banish all evils from thy Church: prosperously guide the steps, actions, and desires of us, and of all thy servants, in the way of salvation: give eternal blessings to our benefactors, and grant everlasting rest to all the faithful departed. Through our Lord Jesus Christ, thy Son, who liveth and reigneth with thee and the Holy Ghost, one God, world without end. *R.* Amen.

(*Commemoration for the Saints in Advent.*)

Antiphona. Ecce Dóminus véniet, et omnes sancti ejus cum eo: et erit in die illa lux magna, allelúia.

Anthem. Behold, the Lord will come, and all his saints with him: and there shall be a great light on that day, allelúia.

V Ecce, apparébit

V. Behold, the Lord

Dóminus in nubem cándidam. R. Et cum eo sanctórum míllia.

shall appear on a bright cloud. R. And with him thousands of saints.

Oremus.

Let us pray.

CONSCIENTIAS nostras quæsumus, Dómine, visitándo puríﬁca, ut veniens Jesus Christus, Fílius tuus, Dóminus noster cum ómnibus sanctis, parátam sibi in nobis invéniat mansiónem: Qui tecum vivit et regnat in unitáte Spíritus Sancti, Deus, per omnia sæcula sæculórum. R. Amen.

CLEANSE our consciences, we beseech thee, O Lord, by thy holy visit, that when Jesus Christ, thy Son, our Lord, cometh with all his saints, he may find in us an abode prepared for his reception: who liveth and reigneth with thee and the Holy Ghost, one God, world without end. R. Amen.

After the commemoration for the Saints, the following Versicles are said, which conclude Vespers.

V. Dómine, exáudi oratiónem meam. R. Et clamor meus ad te véniat.

V. O Lord, hear my prayer. R. And let my cry come unto thee.

Or, as above remarked.

V. Dóminus vobíscum. R. Et cum Spíritu tuo.

V. The Lord be with you. R. And with thy Spirit.

Observe this at the end of each hour.

V. Benedicámus Dómino. R. Deo grátias.

V. Let us bless the Lord. R. Thanks be to God.

V. Fidélium ánimæ per misericórdiam Dei requiéscant in pace. *R.* Amen.

V. May the souls of the faithful departed, through the mercy of God, rest in peace. *R.* Amen.

COMPLIN.

O Divine and adorable Lord Jesus Christ, who hast graciously redeemed us by thy bitter passion and death, we offer up this hour of Complin to thy honour and glory, and most humbly beseech thee, through the injury thou didst suffer by the treacherous kiss of Judas, and by thy capture in the garden, to grant us thy grace, that we may never betray thee by unworthily receiving the blessed Sacraments, particularly the adorable Eucharist of thy body and blood, in the state of mortal sin, and that we may bridle our passions, and bind down our vicious inclinations under the sweet yoke and light burden of thy holy law till death. Amen.

Ave, Maria, &c.

V. Converte nos, Deus, salutáris noster. *R.* Et avérte iram tuam a nobis.

V. Deus, in adjutórium meum inténde. *R.* Dómine, ad adjuvàndum me festína.

Glória Patri, et Fílio, et Spirítui Sancto. Sicut erat in princípio, et nunc, et semper, et in sæcula sæculórum,—

Hail, Mary, &c.

V. Convert us to thee, O God, our Saviour. *R.* And turn away thy wrath from us.

V. Incline unto my aid, O God. *R.* O Lord, make haste to help me.

Glory be to the Father, and to the Son, and to the Holy Ghost. As it was in the beginning, is now, and ever shall

Amen. Allelúia, *vel* Laus tibi, Dómine, rex æternæ glóriæ.

be, world without end, Amen. Alleluia, *or* Praise be to thee, O Lord, king of eternal glory.

Psalmus cxxviii.

Psalm 128.

Sæpe expugnavérunt me á juventúte mea, * dicat nunc Israel.

Many times have they fought against me from my youth, * let Israel now say.

Sæpe expugnavérunt me a juventúte mea: * etenim non potuérunt mihi.

Many times have they fought against me from my youth : * but they could not prevail over me.

Super dorsum meum fabricavérunt peccatóres : * prolongavérunt iniquitátem suam.

The wicked have exerted their cruelty upon my back : * they have prolonged their iniquity.

Dóminus justus concídit cervíces peccatórum : * confundàntur et convertántur retrórsum omnes, qui odérunt Sion.

The Lord, who is just, will cut the necks of sinners : * let them all be confounded and rejected, who hate Sion.

Fiant sicut fœnum tectorum : * quod, priúsquam evellátur, exáruit:

Let them be as grass upon the tops of houses: * which withereth away before it was plucked up:

De quo non implévit manum suam, qui metit : * et sinum suum, qui cólligit.

Wherewith the mower did not fill his hand : * nor the gleaner his bosom.

Et non dixérunt, qui præteríbant: Benedíctio Dómini super vos: * benedíximus vobis in nómine Dómini,

Glória Patri, &c.

Psalmus cxxix.

DE profúndis clamávi ad te Dómine;* Dómine, exáudi vocem meam.

Fiant aures tuæ intendéntes * in vocem deprecationis meæ.

Si iniquitàtes observáveris, Dómine,:* Dómine, quis sustinébit.

Quia apud te propitiátio est: * et propter legem tuam sustínui te Dómine.

Sustínuit ánima mea in verbo ejus: * sperávit ánima mea in Dómine.

A custódia matutína usque ad noctem,* speret Israel in Dómino.

Quia apud Dóminum

And they, who passed by, have not said: The blessing of the Lord be upon you: * we have blessed you in the name of the Lord.

Glory be to the Father.

Psalm 129.

FROM the deep I have cried out to thee; * O gracious Lord, hear my voice.

Let thy ears be attentive * to the voice of my petition.

If thou wilt consider our iniquities, O mighty Lord, * who shall endure it?

But with thee there is merciful forgiveness: * and by reason of thy law I have waited on thee, O Lord.

My soul hath relied on his word: * my soul hath hoped in the Lord.

From the morning watch even until night, * let Israel hope in the Lord.

Because with the Lord

misericórdia : * et copiósa apud eum redémptio.

Et ipse rédimet Israel * ex ómnibus iniquitátibus ejus.

Glória Patri, &c.

Psalmus cxxx.

Domine, non est exaltátum cor meum ;* neque eláti sunt óculi mei.

Neque ambulávi in magnis,* neque in mirabílibus super me.

Si non humiliter sentiébam ; * sed exaltávi ánimam meam:

Sicut ablactátus est super matre sua, * ita retribútio in ánima mea.

Speret Israel in Dómino,* ex hoc nunc, et usque in sæculum.

Glória Patri, &c.

Hymnus.

Memento, rerum Cónditor.

there is mercy: * and with him plentiful redemption.

And he shall redeem Israel * from all his iniquities.

Glory be to the Father.

Psalm 130.

O Lord, my heart is not puffed up: * nor are my eyes disdainful.

Neither have I been ambitious of great affairs, * nor have I dared to scrutinize in wonderful things above me.

If I thought not humbly of myself; * but proudly elevated my mind:

Treat me as a nurse treats her infant, * when she weans it from her breasts.

Let Israel hope in the Lord, * now, and for evermore.

Glory be to the Father.

Hymn.

Remember thou, Creator Lord.

Nostri quod olim córporis,	The Father God's co-equal Word,
Sacráta ab alvo Vírginis	To save mankind, from Virgin's womb
Nascéndo, formam súmpseris.	Our human nature didst assume.
Maria, mater grátiæ,	O happy Mary, full of grace,
Dulcis parens cleméntiæ.	Dear mother of the Prince of Peace,
Tu nos ab hoste prótege,	Protect us from our evil foe,
Et mortis hora súscipe.	And bliss, at death, on us bestow.
Jesu tibi sit glória,	To thee, O Jesus, Mary's Son,
Qui natus es de Vírgine,	Be everlasting homage done;
Cum Patre et almo Spíritu,	To God the Father, we repeat
In sempitérna sæcula. Amen.	The same, and to the Paraclete. Amen.

The Little Chapter through the year, except in Advent:

*Capitulum. Eccli.*xxiv.   *Little Chapter. Ec.* 24.

Ego mater pulchræ dilectiónis, et timóris, et agnitiónis, et sanctæ spei. R. Deo grátias.

I am the mother of beautiful love, and of fear, and of knowledge, and of holy hope. R. Thanks be to God.

V. Ora pro nobis, sancta Dei génitrix. R.

V. Pray for us, O holy mother of God. R. That

Ut digni efficiámur pro-
missiónibus Christi.

Antiphona. Sub tuum
præsidium.

(*Tempore paschali*)
Antiph. Regína cœli.

(*Tempore Nativ.*) *An-
tiph.* Magnum hæredi-
tátis mystérium.

we may be made worthy
of the promises of Christ.

Anthem. Under thy
protection.

(*Paschal time*) *Anth.*
O queen of heaven.

(*Christmas time*) *An-
them.* Great is the mys-
tery of our inheritance.

Little Chapter in Advent, Isaiah 7.

Ecce, virgo concípiet,
et páriet fílium, et vo-
cábitur nomen ejus
Emmánuel. Butyrum
et mel cómedet, ut
sciat reprobáre malum,
et elígere bonum. *R.*
Deo gratias.

Behold, a virgin
shall conceive, and bring
forth a son, and his
name shall be called
Emmanuel. He shall
eat butter and honey,
that he may know how
to reject evil, and choose
good. *R.* Thanks be to
God.

V. Angelus Dómini
nuntiávit Maríæ. *R.*
Et concépit de Spíritu
Sancto.

V. The angel of the
Lord declared unto
Mary. *R.* And she con-
ceived by the Holy
Ghost.

Antiph. Spíritus Sanc-
tus.

Anth. The Holy Ghost.

Canticum Simeonis.
Lucæ ii, xxix.

Canticle of Simeon.
Luke ii, 29.

Nunc dimíttis servum
tuum, Dómine, * se-
cúndum verbum tuum,
in pace :

Now dost thou dis-
miss thy servant, O
Lord, * acccording to
thy word, in peace :

Quia vidérunt óculi mei * salutáre tuum.

Quod parásti * ante fáciem ómnium populórum ;

Lumen ad revelatiónem Géntium, * et glóriam plebis tuæ, Israel.

Glória Patri, &c.

(*Per annum*) *Antiphona.* Sub tuum præsídium confúgimus, sancta Dei génitrix ; nostras deprecatiónes ne despícias in necessitátibus nostris, sed a perículis cunctis líbera nos semper, Virgo gloriósa et benedícta.

(*Tempore paschali*) *Antiphona.* Regína cœli, lætáre, allelúia, quia quem meruísti portáre, allelúia, resurréxit sicut dixit, allelúia : ora pro nobis Deum, allelúia.

(*In Adventu*) *Antiphona.* SpíritusSanctus

Since my eyes have seen * thy promised salvation.

Which thou hast prepared * to shew to all nations :

A light to enlighten the Gentiles, * and the glory of thy people, Israel.

Glory be to the Father, &c.

(*Through the year*) *Anthem.* Under thy protection we seek refuge, O holy mother of God ; despise not our petitions in our necessities, but deliver us continually from all dangers, O glorious and blessed Virgin.

(*In Paschal time*) *Anthem.* O queen of heaven rejoice, alleluia, because he, whom thou didst deserve to bear, alleluia, is risen again, as he foretold, alleluia : pray for us to God, allelui.

(*In Advent*) *Anthem.* The Holy Ghost shall

in te descéndet María: ne tímeas, habebis in útero Fílium Dei, allelúia.

(*Tempore Nativ.*) *Antiphona.* Magnum hæreditátis mystérium: templum Dei factus est úterus nesciéntis virum: non est pollútus ex ea carnem assúmens: omnes gentes vénient dicéntes: Glória tibi, Dómine.

Kyrie eléison. Christe eléison. Kyrie eléison.

V. Dómine exáudi oratiónem meam. Et clamor meus ad te véniat.

Oremus.

(*Per annum*) BEATÆ et gloriósæ semper Vírginis Maríæ, quæsumus, Dómine intercéssio gloriósa nos prótegat, et ad vitam perdúcat ætérnam. Per Dóminum nostrum, Jesum Christum, Filium tuum, qui tecum vivit et regnat in

come upon thee, Mary: do not fear, thou shalt have in thy womb the Son of God, alleluia.

(*Christmas time*) *Anthem.* Great is the mystery of our inheritance: the womb of a pure virgin became the temple of God: he, who took flesh of her, was not defiled: all nations shall come and say: Glory be to thee, O Lord.

Lord, have mercy on us. Christ, have mercy on us. Lord, have mercy on us.

V. O Lord, hear my prayer. R. And let my cry come unto thee.

Let us pray.

(*Through the year*) GRANT, we beseech thee, O Lord, that the glorious intercession of the ever blessed and glorious Virgin Mary may protect us here, and bring us to everlasting life. Through our Lord, Jesus Christ, thy Son:

unitàte Spíritus Sancti, Deus, per ómnia sæcula sæculórum. R. Amen.

(*In Adventu*) DEUS, qui de beátæ Maríæ Vírginis útero verbum tuum, Angelo nuntiánte, carnem suscípere voluíste; præsta supplícibus tuis, ut, qui verè eam genitrícem Dei crédimus, ejus apud te intercessiónibus ad juvémur. Per eundem Dominum nostrum, Jesum Christum, &c.

(*Tempore Nativ.*)— DEUS, qui salútis ætérnæ beátæ Maríæ virginitáte fœcúnda humáno géneri præmia præstitísti; tríbue, quæsumus, ut ipsam pro nobis intercédere sentiámus, per quam merúimus auctórem vitæ suscípere, Dóminum nostrum Jesum Christum, Fílium tuum: Qui tecum vivet et regnat in unitáte Spíritus, &c.

Who, with thee and the Holy Ghost, liveth and reigneth one God, world without end. R. Amen.

(*In Advent*) O GOD, who wast pleased that thy word, when the Angel delivered his message, should take flesh in the womb of the blessed Virgin Mary; give ear to our humble petitions, and grant that we, who believe her to be truly the mother of God, may be helped by her prayers. Through the same Lord, Jesus Christ, &c.

(*Christmas time*) O GOD, who, by the fruitful virginity of blessed Mary, has given to mankind the rewards of eternal salvation; grant, we beseech thee, that we may experience her intercession, by whom we have deserved to receive the Author of life, our Lord, Jesus Christ, thy Son: Who with thee and the Holy Ghost, liveth, &c.

V. Dómine, exáudi oratiónem meam. *R.* Et clamor meus ad te véniat.

V. Benedicámus Dómino. *R.* Deo grátias.

Benedictio. Benedícat et custódiat nos omnípotens et miséricors Dóminus, Pater, et Fílius, et Spíritus Sanctus. *R.* Amen.

V. O Lord, hear my prayer. *R.* And let my cry come unto thee.

V. Let us bless the Lord. *R.* Thanks be to God.

Blessing. May the almighty and merciful Lord, the Father, the Son, and the Holy Ghost, bless and protect us. *R.* Amen.

Then is said one of the following Anthems, according to the time of the year:

The Anthem from Vespers of Saturday before the first Sunday of Advent, till Vespers on the Feast of the Purification, 2d of February.

Alma Redemptóris mater quæ pérvia cœli,
Porta manes, et stella maris, succúrre cadenti,
Súrgere qui curat, pópulo: tu quæ genuísti,
Natúra miránte, tuum sanctum Genitórem:
Virgo priùs ac pestériùs, Gabriélis ab ore.

Sumens illud Ave, peccatórum miserére.

Mother of Jesus, heaven's open gate,
Star of the sea, support the falling state
Of mortals: thou, whose womb thy Maker bore,
And yet, O strange! a virgin as before:
Who didst from Gabriel's hail the news receive,
Repenting sinners by thy prayers relieve.

V. Angelus Dómini nuntiávit Maríæ. *R.* Et concépit de Spíritu Sancto.

Oremus.

Gratiam tuam, quæsumus, Dómine, méntibus nostris infúnde: ut qui Angelo nuntiánte Christi, Fílii tui, incarnatiónem cognóvimus, per passiónem ejus et crucem ad resurrectiónis glóriam perducámur: Per eúndem Christum Dóminum nostrum. Amen.

V. The angel of the Lord declared unto Mary. *R.* And she conceived by the Holy Ghost.

Let us pray.

Pour forth, we beseech thee, O Lord, thy grace into our hearts, that we, to whom the incarnation of Christ, thy Son, was made known by the message of an angel, may by his passion and cross be brought to the glory of his resurrection: Through the same Christ, our Lord. Amen.

From Vigil of Christmas the above Versicle and Prayer are changed, thus:—

V. Post partum virgo inviolāta permansísti.— *R.* Dei génitrix, intercéde pro nobis.

Oremus.

Deus, qui sālútis ætérnæ beátæ Maríæ virginitáti fœcúnda humano géneri præmia præstitísi; tríbue quæsumus, ut ipsum pro nobis in-

V. After child-birth thou didst remain a pure virgin. *R.* O Mother of God, intercede for us.

Let us pray.

O God, who by the fruitful virginity of blessed Mary, hast given to mankind the rewards of eternal salvation, grant, we beseech thee, that we

tercédere sentiámus, per quam merúimus auctórem vitæ suscípere, Dóminum nostrum, Jesum Christum, Fílium tuum. Amen.

may experience her intercession, by whom we received the Author of life, our Lord, Jesus Christ, thy Son. Amen.

The Anthem from Complin on the Feast of the Purification inclusively, till None on Holy Saturday :—

Ave, Regína cœlórum!

Ave, dómina angelórum!

Salve radix! salve porta!

Ex qua mundo lux est orta.

Gaude, Virgo gloriósa,

Super omnes speciósa!

Vale, O valde decóra!

Et pro nobis Christum exora.

V. Dignáre me laudáre te, Virgo sacráta. *R.* Da mihi virtútem contra hostes tuos.

Oremus.

Concede, miséricors Deus, fragilitáti nostræ

Hail Mary, Queen of heavenly spheres!

Hail, whom th' angelic host reveres!

Hail, fruitful root! Hail, sacred gate,

From whom our light derives its date.

O glorious Maid, with beauty blest!

May joys eternal fill thy breast!

Thus crown'd with beauty and with joy,

Thy prayers for us with Christ employ.

V. Vouchsafe, O sacred Virgin, to accept my praises. *R.* Give me strength against thy enemies.

Let us pray.

Grant us, O merciful God, strength against

præsídium; ut qui sanctæ Dei genitrícis memóriam ágimus intercessiónis ejus auxílio a nostris iniquitátibus resurgámus : Per eúndem Christum Dóminum nostrum. Amen.

all our weakness; that we, who celebrate the memory of the holy Mother of God, may by the help of her intercession rise again from our iniquities : Through the same Christ, our Lord. Amen.

The Anthem from Vespers on Holy Saturday till None on Saturday in Whitsun-week :—

REGINA cœli lætáre, allelúia,

Quia quem meruísti portáre, allelúia,
Resurréxit sicut dixit, allelúia :
Ora pro nobis Deum, allelúia.

REJOICE, O Queen of heaven, to see, alleluia,

The sacred infant born of thee, alleluia,
Return in glory from the tomb, alleluia :
And with thy prayers prevent our doom, alleluia.

V. Gaude et lætáre, Virgo María, allelúia.
R. Quia surréxit Dóminus verè, alleluia.

V. Rejoice and exult, O Virgin Mary, alleluia.
R. For the Lord is truly risen, alleluia.

Oremus.

DEUS, qui per resurrectiónem Fílii tui, Domini nostri, Jesu Christi, mundum lætificáre dignátus es; præsta, quæsumus, ut, per ejus

Let us pray.

O GOD, who by the resurrection of thy Son, our Lord, Jesus Christ, hast been pleased to fill the world with joy : grant, we beseech thee,

genitrícem Vírginem Maríam, perpétuæ capiámus gáudia vitæ: Per eúndem Christum, Dónum, nostrum. Amen.

that by the intercession of the Virgin Mary, his mother, we may receive the joys of eternal life: Thro' the same Christ, our Lord. Amen.

The Anthem from Vespers on the Eve of the most Sacred Trinity till None on Saturday before the first Sunday of Advent.

SALVE, Regína, mater misericórdiæ!

HAIL, happy Queen, thou mercy's parent, hail!

Vita, dulcédo, et spes nostra, salve!
Ad te clamámus, éxules fílii Hevæ.

Life, hope, and comfort of this earthly vale,
To thee we, Eva's wretched children, cry,

Ad te suspirámus, geméntes et flentes in hac lacrymárum valle.
Eja ergo, advocáta nostra!
Illos tuos misericórdes óculos ad nos convérte.
Et Jesum, benedíctum fructum ventris tui, nobis post hoc exílium osténde.
O clemens, O pia, O dulcis Virgo Maria.
V. Ora pro nobis

In sighs and tears, to thee we suppliants fly.

Rise, glorious advocate, exert thy love,
And let our vows those eyes of pity move.

O pious Virgin Mary, grant that we,

Long exiled, may in heaven thy Jesus see.
V. Pray for us, O ho-

sancta Dei génitrix. *R.* Ut digni efficiámur promissiónibus Christi.

ly Mother of God. *R.* That we may be made worthy of the promises of Christ.

Oremus.

Let us pray.

OMNIPOTENS sempitérne Deus, qui gloriósæ Virginis Matris Mariæ corpus et ánimam, ut dignum Fílii tui habitáculum éffici mererétur, Spíritu Sancto cooperánte, preparásti; da, ut cujus commemoratióne lætámur, ejus pia intercessióne ab instántibus malis et á morte perpétua liberémur: Per eúndem Christum, Dominum nostrum.— Amen.

O ALMIGHTY and eternal God, who by the co-operation of the Holy Ghost, didst prepare the body and soul of the glorious Virgin Mary, that she might become a habitation worthy of thy Son; grant that, as with joy we celebrate her memory, so by her pious intercession we may be delivered from present evils and eternal death: Thro' the same Christ, our Lord. Amen.

After the proper Anthem of the blessed Virgin Mary, according to the time of the year, is said the Versicle.

V. Divínum auxílium máneat semper nobiscum. *R.* Amen.

V. May the divine assistance always remain with us. *R.* Amen.

Pater Noster, Ave Maria, *and* Credo, *are here said in secret; but in the other parts of the Office, in the end of the last Hour,* Pater Noster *only is said.*

☞ *In all the hours of the Office, except Complin, the following Versicle is said immediately before the foregoing Anthems:*—

V. Domine, exáudi nationem meam. R. Et clamor meus ad te veniat.

V. O Lord, hear my prayer. R. And let my cry come unto thee.

MATINS, WITH LAUDS.

O DIVINE and adorable Lord, Jesus Christ, who hast graciously redeemed us by thy bitter passion and death, we offer up these Matins and Lauds to thy honour and glory, and most humbly beseech thee, through the vile treatment thou didst receive from the Jews, who dragged thee to the courts of impious High Priests, where thou wast falsely accused, smote on the face, called a blasphemer, and declared guilty of death, and didst suffer most cruel torments with blows, bruises, and unheard of injuries, during the whole night, to grant us resignation and silence under all calumnies, detractions, and sufferings, for the love of thee, and to give us grace never to return injury for injury, but to practise that truly Christian revenge of overcoming evil with good, to do good to those who hate us, to bless those who curse us, and to pray for those who persecute and calumniate us. Amen.

Ave María, &c.

V. Dómine, lábia mea apéries. R. Et os meum annuntiábit laudem tuam.

V. Deus, in adjutórium meum inténde. R. Dómine, ad adjuvándum me festína.

Glória Patri, et Fílio, et Spirítui Sancto. Si-

Hail Mary, &c.

V. O Lord, open thou my lips. R. And my mouth shall declare thy praise.

V. Incline unto my aid, O God. R. O Lord, make haste to help me.

Glory be to the Father, and to the Son,

MATINS.

cut erat in princípio, et
nunc, et semper, et in
sæcula sæculórum.—
Amen, Allelúia, *vel*
Laus tibi, Dómine, rex
ætérnæ glóriæ.

and to the Holy Ghost.
As it was in the beginning, is now, and ever
shall be, world without
end. Amen, Alleluia,
or Praise be to thee, O
Lord, king of eternal
glory.

Invitatorium.

Ave, María, grátia
plena, Dóminus tecum.

Ave, María, grátia
plena, Dóminus tecum.

Invitatory.

Hail, Mary, full of
grace, the Lord is with
thee.

Hail, Mary, full of
grace, the Lord is with
thee.

Psalmus xciv.

VENITE, exultémus
Dómino, jubilémus Deo
salutári nostro: præoccupémus fáciem ejus in
confessióne, et in psalmis
jubilémus ei.

Psalm 94.

COME, let us rejoice
in the Lord, let us joyfully cry out to God
our Saviour; let us present ourselves before
him, to celebrate his
praises, and to sing with
joy canticles unto him.

Ave, María, grátia
plena, Dóminus tecum.

Hail, Mary, full of
grace, the Lord is with
thee.

Quóniam Deus magnus Dóminus, et Rex
magnus super omnes
deos; quónium non repéllet Dóminus plebem
suam, quia in manu ejus

Because God is a
mighty Lord and a
great King above all
gods; for the Lord will
not reject his people;
in his hand are all the

sunt omnes fines terræ, et altitúdines móntium ipse cónspicit.

Dóminus tecum.

Quónium ipsíus est mare, et ipse fecit illud, et áridam fundavérunt manus ejus: veníte, adorémus, et procedámus ante Deum: plorémus coram Domino, qui fecit nos: quia ipse est Dominus Deus noster, nos autem populus ejus, et oves pascuæ ejus.

Ave, María, grátia plena: Dominus tecum.

Hodie si vocem ejus audiéritis, nolíte obduráre corda vestra, sicut in exacerbátione secúndum diem tentationis in deserto: ubi tentavérunt me patres vestri, probavérunt, et vidérunt opera mea.

Dominus tecum.

Quadraginta annis proximus fui generati-

bounds of the earth, and he looks down on the heights of the mountains.

The Lord is with thee.

The sea is his; for he made it, and his hands framed the earth; come then let us adore, and fall prostrate before God, let us weep in the presence of the Lord, who made us, because he is the Lord our God; we are his people, and the sheep of his pasture.

Hail, Mary, full of grace, the Lord is with thee.

If this day you should hear his voice, harden not your hearts, as you did, when you provoked him on the day you offended him in the desert; where your fathers tempted me, they tried, and saw my works.

The Lord is with thee.

I was forty years with this race of men,

oni huic, et dixi: Semper hi érrant corde; ipsi vero non cognoverunt vias meas, quibus jurávi in ira mea si introíbunt in requiem meam.

Ave María, gratia plena: Dominus tecum.

Gloria Patri et Filio, et Spiritui Sancto. Sicut erat in principio, et nunc, et semper, et in sæcula sæculorum.— Amen.

Dominus tecum.
Ave María, gratia plena,
Dominus tecum.

Hymnus.

Quem terra, pontus, Sidera
Colunt, adorant prædicant,
Trinem regentem machinam,
Claustram Mariæ bajulat.

and said: The hearts of this people are always wandering; but they have not known my ways; and I swore to them in my wrath, that they should not enter my abode of rest.

Hail, Mary, full of grace, the Lord is with thee.

Glory be to the Father, and to the Son, and to the Holy Ghost. As it was in the beginning, is now, and ever shall be, world without end. Amen.

The Lord is with thee.
Hail, Mary, full of grace.
The Lord is with thee.

Hymn.

The sov'reign God, whose hands sustain
The globe of heav'n, the earth and main,
Ador'd and praised by each degree,
Lies hid, O sacred Maid, in thee.

Cui luna, sol, et omnia	HE, whom the sun and moon obey,
Deserviunt per témpora,	To whom all creatures homage pay;
Perfúsa cœli gratia	The Judge of men and angels' doom
Gestant puéllæ viscera.	Resides within thy virgin womb.
Beata Mater munere,	O HAPPY parent, chose to bear
Cujus, supernus Artifex	Thy Maker's co-eternal Heir;
Mundum pugíllo continens,	Whose fingers span this earth around,
Ventris sub arca clausus est.	Whose arms the whole creation bound.
Beata cœli Nuncio,	THE angel's voice pronounc'd thee blest,
Fæcúnda sancto Spiritu,	The Holy Ghost on thee did rest;
Desiderátus gentibus,	To us thou didst bestow by birth
Cujus per alvum fusus est.	The most desir'd of heav'n and earth.
Jesu, tibi sit gloria,	To thee, O Jesus, Mary's Son,
Qui natus es de Virgine,	Be everlasting homage done;
Cum Patre, et almo Spiritu,	To God the Father we repeat
In sempiterna sæcula. Amen.	The same, and to the Paraclete. Amen.

MATINS.

☞ *The three following Psalms are said on Sundays, Mondays, and Thursdays, at the Nocturn:—*

Antiphona. Benedicta tu.	*Anthem.* Blessed art thou.
Psalmus viii.	*Psalm* 8.
Domine Dominus noster, * quam admirábile est nomen tuum in universa terra.	O Lord, our sovereign Lord, * how wonderful is thy name over the whole earth!
Quoniam elevata est magnificéntia tua * super cœlos.	For thy grandeur is exalted * above the heavens.
Ex ore infántium et lacténtium perfecísti laudem propter inimícos tuos, * ut déstruas inimícum et ultorem.	Thou hast received due praise from the mouths of infants and of sucklings, to confound thy enemies, * and to destroy the spirit of hatred and of vengeance.
Quoniam videbo cœlos tuos, opera dignitorum tuorum : * lunam et stellas, quæ tu fundasti.	For I shall consider the heavens; which are the work of thy hands: * the moon and stars, which thou hast formed.
Quid est homo, quod memor es ejus! * aut filius hominis, quoniam visitas eum.	What is man, that thou art mindful of him? * or the son of man, that thou dost visit him?
Minuisti eum paulo	Thou hast created

minus ab Angelis, gloria et honore coronásti eum : * et constituísti eum super opera manuum tuarum.

Omnia subjecísti sub pedibus ejus, * oves et boves univérsas, ínsuper et pécora campi ?

Volucres cœli, et pisces maris, * qui perámbulant sémitas maris.

Domine Dominus noster, * quam admirabile est nomen tuum in universa terra !

Gloria Patria, &c.

Antiphona. Benedícta tu in muliéribus, et benedíctus fructus ventris tui.

Antiph. Sicut myrrha elécta.

Psalmus xviii.

Cœli enàrrant gloriam Dei,* et ópera mánuum

him a little inferior to the angels, thou hast crowned him with honour and glory: and gave him dominion over all the works of thy hands.

Thou hast rendered all things subject to him, * the sheep, and the oxen, and also the cattle of the field.

The birds of the air, and the fishes of the sea, * and all that glide through the course of the waters.

O Lord, our Sovereign Lord, * how wonderful is thy name over the whole earth.

Glory be to the Father.

Anthem. Blessed art thou among women : and blessed is the fruit of thy womb.

Anth. Like choice myrrh.

Psalm 18.

The heavens display the glory of God, * and

ejus annúntiat firmaméntum.

Dies diéi erúctat verbum,* et nox nocti indicat sciéntiam.

Non sunt loquélæ, neque sermónes; * quorum non audiántur voces eórum.

In omnem terram exívit sonus eórum : * et in fines orbis terræ verba eórum.

In sole pósuit tabernáculum suum : * et ipse tamquam sponsus procédens de thálamo suo :

Exultávit ut gigas ad curréndam viam : * á summo cœlo egréssio ejus :

Et occúrsus ejus usque ad summum ejus; * nec est qui se abscóndat á calóre ejus.

Lex Dómini immacu-

the firmament publish the works of his hands.

Each day announces his word to the following day, * and each night declares his knowledge to the succeeding night.

There are no tongues or languages, * where their voices are not heard.

Their eloquence went forth through the whole world, * and their words have reached the bounds of the earth.

The glory of his abode is fulgent like the Sun, * and he is adorned like the bridegroom going out of his chamber.

He proceeded with joy like a giant on his way ; * his coming forth begins from the summit of heaven.

And he continues his course to the end thereof : * there is not one, who can abscond from his rays.

The law of the Lord

láta, convértens ánimas : * testimónium Dómini fidéle, sapiéntiam præstans párvulis.

Justítiæ Dómini rectæ, lætificántes corda :* præcéptum Dómini lúcidum, illúminans óculos.

Timor Dómini sanctus, pérmanens in sæculum sæculi : * judicia Dómini vera, justificáta in semétipsa.

Desiderabília super aurum et lápidem pretiósum multum : * et dulcióra super mel et favum.

Etenim servus tuus custódit ea : * in custodiéndis illis retribútio multa.

Delícta quis intélligit? ab occúltis meis munda me,* et ab aliénis parce servo tuo.

is perfect, it converts souls : * the words of the Lord are faithful, and give wisdom to the humble.

The ordinances of the Lord are righteous, rejoicing the hearts : * the precept of the Lord is luminous, and enlightens our understanding.

The fear of the Lord is holy, and continues for evermore : * the judgments of the Lord are founded on truth and justice.

They are more desirable than gold or precious stones ; * and sweeter than the honey, and honey-comb.

For thy servant observeth them ; * and they who keep them find an ample recompense.

Who can comprehend what sin is ? Cleanse me from my hidden sins, * and from those of others save thy servant.

Si mei non fúerint dominâti, tunc immaculátus ero : * et emundabor á delícto máximo.

Et erunt ut compláceant elóquia oris mei : * et meditátio cordis mei in conspéctu tuo semper.

Dómine adjútor meus, * et redémptor meus.

Glória Patri, &c.

Antiphona. Sicut myrrha elécta odórem dedisti suavitàtis sancta Dei génitrix.

Antiph. Ante torum hujus virginis.

Psalmus xxiii.

DOMINI est terra, et plenitúdo ejus; * orbis terrárum, et univérsi qui hábitant in eo.

Quia ipse super mária fundávit eum; * et super flúmina præparávit eum.

If they shall not be imputed to me, I will be then pure, * and will be free from the very great guilt of sin.

Then shall my prayer be directed to please thee : * and my interior meditation be always made in thy presence.

O Lord, thou art my help, * and my Redeemer.

Glory be to the Father.

Anthem. Like choice myrrh, thou hast rendered a most fragrant odour, O holy mother of God.

Anth. In honour of this most chaste virgin.

Psalm 23.

THE Lord possesses the earth, and all that it contains : * he owns the whole world, and all its inhabitants.

For he hath founded it on the seas; * and hath raised it over the surface of the rivers.

Quis ascóndet in montem Dómini? * aut quis stabit in loco sancto ejus?

Innocens mánibus, et mundo corde, * qui non accépit in vano ánimam suam, nec jurávit in dolo próximo suo:

Hic accípiet benedictionem á Dómino, * et misericórdiam á Deo salutári suo.

Hæc est generátio quæréntium eum,* quæréntium fáciem Dei Jacob.

Attóllite portas príncipes vestras et elevámini portæ æternáles:* et introíbit Rex glóriæ?

Quis est iste Rex glóriæ? * Dóminus fortis et potens, Dóminus potens in prælio.

Attóllite portas príncipes vestras, et elevá-

Who shall ascend on the mount of the Lord?* and who shall dwell in his holy sanctuary?

Thóse, who do no harm, and are pure of heart; * who do not give their heart to vain desires, nor deceive his neighbour by false oaths.

He shall receive the blessing of the Lord, * and mercy from God, his Saviour.

Such is the inheritance of those, who truly seek him, * who desire the presence of the God of Jacob.

Open wide your gates, O ye princes, let the eternal doors be thrown open, * and the King of glory shall make his entrance.

Who is this King of glory? * he is the valiant and mighty Lord, the Lord who has triumphed in battle.

Open wide your gates, O ye princes, let the

mini portæ æternáles :* et introíbit Rex glóræ.

eternal gates be thrown open,* and the King of glory shall make his entrance.

Quis est iste Rex glóriæ? * Dóminus virtútum ipse est Rex glóriæ.

Who is the King of glory? * the Lord of hosts is this king of glory.

Glória Patri, &c.

Glory be to the Father.

Antiphona. Ante torum hujus vírginis frequentate nobis dúlcia cántica drámatis.

Anthem. In honour of this most chaste virgin, let us sing canticles with sweet harmony.

V. Diffúsa est grátia in lábiis tuis. *R.* Proptéreà benedíxit te Deus in ætérnum.

V. Grace is spread on thy lips. *R.* Therefore God hath blessed thee for ever.

Pater noster.

Our Father.

The Absolution, Benedictions, Lessons, and Responsories, are set down below after the Psalms, p. 67.

The three following Psalms are said on Tuesdays and Fridays at the Nocturn.

Antiphona. Spécie tua.

Anthem. In thy comeliness.

Psalmus xliv.

Psalm 44.

Eructavit cor meum verbum bonum :* dico ego ópera mea regi.

My heart is ready to declare grand things : * I will devote my works to the King of kings.

Lingua mea cálamus

My tongue shall fol-

scribæ, * velóciter scribéntis.

Speciósus forma præ fíliis hóminum, diffúsa est grátia in lábiis tuis ; * proptéreà benedíxit te Deus in ætérnum.

Accíngere gládio tuo super femur tuum, * Potentissime.

Spécie tua et pulchritúdine tua, * inténde, prospere procede et regna.

Propter veritátem, et mansuetúdinem, et justitiam : * et dedúcet te mirabiliter déxtera tua.

Saggíttæ tuæ acútæ, populi sub te cadent : * in corda inimicórum regis.

Sedes tua Deus in sæculum sæculi : * virga directiónis virga regni tui.

Dilexísti justítiam, et odísti iniquitátem : *

low his inspiration, * like the quick pen of an able scrivener.

O thou most beautiful among the sons of men, grace is spread on thy lips ; * therefore God hath blessed thee for ever.

Gird thyself with thy sword, * O thou most Mighty.

In thy comeliness and thy beauty, * go on, proceed prosperously, and reign.

For the sake of truth, of meekness, and of justice : * and thy right hand shall conduct thee wonderfully.

Thy arrows are sharp, under thee shall people fall : * they shall pierce the hearts of the king's enemies.

Thy throne, O God, is an eternal reign : * the sceptre of thy empire is a sceptre of equity.

Thou hast loved justice, and hated iniqui-

proptérea unxit te Deus, Deus tuus óleo lætítiæ præ consórtibus tuis.

Myrrha, et gutta, et cásia à vestiméntis tuis, à dómibus ebúrneis: * ex quibus delectavérunt te fíliæ regum in honóre tuo.

Astitit regína à dextris tuis in vestítu deauráto, * circúmdata varietáte.

Audi fília, et vide, inclína aurem tuam: * et obliviscere pópulum tuum, et domum patris tui.

Et concupíscet rex decórum tuum: quóniam ipse est Dóminus Deus tuus, et adorabunt eum.

Et filiæ Tyri in munéribus * vultum tuum deprecabúnter omnes divites plebis.

Omnis glória ejus fíliæ regis ab intus, *

ty; * therefore the Lord thy God, anointed thee with the oil of joy above all thy partners.

Myrrh, and aloes, and cassia, perfume thy robes, and thy ivory palaces: * where the daughters of the king have the honour to entertain thee.

The queen on thy right hand in vesture trimmed with gold, * and variegated with ornaments.

Hearken my daughter, and see, and incline thy ear, * forget thy people, and thy father's house.

And the king will be enamoured with thy beauty, * for he is the Lord thy God, and the people will adore him.

And the daughters of Tyre shall offer gifts, * yea the rich nobility too will come to render thee their vows.

All the glory of the king's daughter is in

in fímbriis áureis circumamícta varietátibus.

Adducéntur regi vírgines post eam : * próximæ ejus afferéntur tibi :

Afferéntur in lætítia et exultatióne : * adducéntur in templum regis.

Pro pátribus tuis nati sunt tibi fílii : * constítues eos príncipes super omnem terram.

Mémores erunt nóminis tui * in omni generatióne et generatiónem.

Proptéreà pópuli confitebúntur tibi in ætérnum, * et in sæculum sæculi.

Glória Patri, &c.

Antiphona. Spécie tua, et pulchritúdine

her interior ; * although she be decorated with fringes of gold and embroideries.

Virgins shall be conducted in her retinue to the king : * her neighbours shall be brought to thee.

They shall be accompanied with joy and delights : * and shall be introduced into the temple of the king.

Thou art blessed with children to hold the place of thy fathers : * thou wilt appoint them princes over the whole earth.

They shall be mindful of thy name, * through succession of ages.

Therefore shall the people praise thee for ever, * yea for evermore.

Glory be to the Father, &c.

Anthem. In thy comeliness and thy

tua inténde, prosperé procéde, et regna.

Antiph. Adjuvábit eam Deus.

Psalmus xlv.

Deus noster refúgium, et virtus : * adjutor in tribulatiónibus, quæ invenérunt nos nimis.

Proptéreá non timébimus dum turbábitur terra, * et transferéntur montes in cor maris.

Sonuérunt, et turbátæ sunt aquæ eórum : * conturbáti sunt montes in fortitúdine ejus.

Flúminis ímpetus lætificat civitàtem Dei : * sanctificávit tabernáculum suum Altissimus.

Deus in médio ejus, non commovébitur : * adjuvábit eam Deus mané dilúculó.

Conturbátæ sunt Gen-

beauty, go on, proceed prosperously, and reign.

Anth. God will assist her.

Psalm 45.

God is our refuge and strength : * he is our helper in afflictions, which have heavily fallen on us.

So we shall have nothing to fear, when the earth will be troubled, * and the mountains transported into the depth of the sea.

The waters roared, and were disturbed ; * and their impetuous torrent made the mountains tremble.

A current of heavenly joy overflows the city of God : * the Most High hath sanctified his own tabernacle.

God is in the midst thereof, it shall not be disturbed : * the Lord will protect it from the dawn of the morning.

Nations are disturb-

tes, et inclináta sunt regna: * dedit vocem suam, mota est terra.

Dóminus virtútum nobíscum: * suscéptor noster Deus Jacob.

Veníte, et vidéte ópera Dómini, quæ pósuit prodígia super terram: * áuferens bella usque ad finem terræ.

Arcum cónteret et confrínget arma: * et scuta combúret igni:

Vacáte, et vidéte quóniam ego sum Deus: * exaltábor in Géntibus, et exaltábor in terra.

Dóminus virtútum nobíscum: * suscéptor noster Deus Jacob.

Glória Patri, &c.

Antiphona. Adjuvábit eam Deus vultu suo: Deus in médio ejus, non commovébitur.

Antiph. Sicut lætántium ómnium.

ed, and kingdoms have tottered: * the earth trembled at his voice.

The Lord of hosts is with us: * the God of Jacob is our protector.

Come, and behold the works of the Lord, and the prodigies he wrought on earth: * he makes the wars cease, even to the bounds of the earth.

He shall destroy the bow, and break the weapons: and cast the shields into the fire.

Consider, and know that I am the Lord; * I shall rule over nations, and shall be great on earth.

The Lord of hosts is with us: * the God of Jacob is our protector.

Glory be to the Father, &c.

Anthem. God will assist her with his presence. God is in the midst of her, she shall not be disturbed.

Anth. All shall truly rejoice.

MATINS.

Psalmus lxxxvi.

Fundamenta ejus in móntibus sanctis : * díligit Dóminus portas Sion super ómnia tabernácula Jacob.

Gloriósa dicta sunt de te, * cívitas Dei.

Memor ero Rahab et Babylonis, * sciéntium me.

Ecce alienígenæ, et Tyrus, et pópulus Ethiopum ; * hi fuérunt illic.

Numquid Sion dicet : Homo, et homo natus est in ea : * et ipse fundávit eam Altíssimus ?

Dóminus narrábit in scriptúris populòrum, et príncipum ; * horum, qui fuérunt in ea.

Sicut lætántium ómnium * habitátio est in te.
Glória Patri, &c.

Antiphona. Sicut lætántium ómnium nos-

Psalm 86.

Sion is founded on holy mountains, * the Lord is pleased with its gates above all the tabernacles of Jacob.

Glorious things are spoken of thee, O city of God.

I shall be mindful of Rahab, and Babylon, * to whom I will make myself known.

Behold the Philistines and Tyre, and the inhabitants of Ethiopia : * these shall be there.

Shall not Sion say : A man is born in her, and this man is the Most High, who founded her ?

The Lord shall relate in the records of the people and of princes, * the names of those, who have dwelt therein.

All shall truly rejoice, * who abide in thee.
Glory be to the Father, &c.

Anthem. We all shall truly rejoice, if we are

trum habitátio est in te, sancta Dei génetrix.

constantly devoted to thee, O holy mother of God.

V. Diffúsa est grátia in lábiis tuis. *R.* Proptéreá benedíxit te Deus in ætérnum.

V. Grace is spread on thy lips. *R.* Therefore God hath blessed thee for ever.

Pater nostér.

Our Father.

The Absolution, Benedictions, Lessons, and Responsories, are set down below, after the Psalms, p. 67.

The three following Psalms are said on Wednesdays and Saturdays at the Nocturn:—

Antiphona. Gaude, María Virgo.

Anthem. Rejoice, O Virgin Mary,

Psalmus xcv.

Psalm 95.

CANTATE Dómino cánticum novum: * cantáte Dómino omnis terra.

SING to the Lord a new canticle: * let the whole earth chaunt the praises of the Lord.

Cantáte Domino, et benedícite Domini ejus: * annuntiáte de die in diem salutáre ejus.

Sing to the Lord, and bless his holy name: * proclaim each day the good tidings of salvation.

Annuntiáte inter Gentes glóriam ejus, * in ómnibus pópulis mirabília ejus.

Publish his glory among the Gentiles, * and his wonderful works among the people.

Quóniam magnus Dóminus, et laudábilis nimis : * terríbilis est super omnes deos.

For the Lord is great, and most worthy of all praise : * he is to be feared above all the gods of the earth.

Quóniam omnes dii Géntium dæmónia : * Dóminus autem cœlos fecit.

Conféssio et pulchritúdo in conspéctu ejus: * sanctimónia et magnificéntia in sanctificatióne ejus.

Afférte Dómino pátriæ Géntium, afferte Dómino glóriam et honórem : * afférte Dómino glóriam nómini ejus.

Tóllite hóstias, et introíte in átria ejus : * adoráte Dóminum in átrio sancto ejus.

Commoveátur á fácie ejus univérsa terra : * dícite in Géntibus, quia Dóminus regnàvit.

Etenim corréxit orbem terræ, qui non commovebitur : * judicábit pópulos in æquitáte.

Lætèntur cœli, et ex-

Because all the gods of the Gentiles are devils : * but our Lord has formed the heavens above.

Glory and beauty belong to him ; * holiness and grandeur decorate his sanctuary.

Bring to the Lord, ye kindred of the Gentiles, render to the Lord glory and honor : * give that glory due to the name of the Lord.

Prepare sacrifices, and enter into his courts. * adore the Lord in his holy sanctuary.

Let the earth be moved at his presence : * announce it to the nations : Behold, the Lord reigneth.

For he hath established order on the earth, which shall not be disturbed : * the Lord will judge all people according to the truth of his holy law.

May the heavens re-

ultet terra, commoveátur mare, et plenitúdo ejus : * gaudébunt campi, et ómnia quæ in eis sunt.

joice, and may the earth, the sea, and all its fullness exult in transports of joy : * may the country around, and what it contains, be animated with gladness.

Tunc exultàbunt ómnia ligna silvárum á fácie Dómini, quia venit :* quóniam venit judicáre terram.

Then shall all the trees of the forests be revested with delight before the presence of the Lord, because he cometh : * for he is come to judge the earth.

Judicàbit orbem terræ in æquitàte, * et pópulos in veritáte sua.

He will judge the world with justice, * and all the people according to the truth of his holy law.

Glória Patri, &c.

Glory be to the Father, &c.

Antiphona. Gaude, Maria Virgo, cunctas hæresses sola interemísti in univérso mundo.

Anthem. Rejoice, O virgin Mary, thou alone hast rendered the church triumphant over all the heresies spread through the earth.

Antiph. Dignáre me laudáre te.

Anth. Vouchsafe that I may praise thee.

Psalmus xcvi.

Psalm 96.

Dominus regnávit,

The Lord hath reign-

exúltet terra : * lœténtur ínsulæ multæ.

Nubes et calígo in circúitu ejus : * justítia et judícium corréctio sedis ejus.

Ignis ante ipsum præcédit, * et inflammábit in circúitu inimícos ejus.

Illuxérunt fúlgura ejus orbi terræ : * vidit, et commóta est terra.

Montes sicut cera fluxérunt á fácie Dómini ; * á fácie Dómini omnis terra.

Annuntiavérunt cœli justítiam ejus : * et vidérunt omnes pópuli glóriam ejus.

Confundántur omnes, qui adórant sculptília :* et qui gloriántur in simulácris suis.

Adoráte eum omnes

ed, let the earth rejoice : * and may gladness be spread through many islands.

Clouds of darkness are around him : * justice and equity are the basis of his throne.

A flame of fire shall precede him, * and shall consume around all his enemies.

His lightnings flash throughout the world :* the earth saw the light, and was moved to fear.

The mountains have melted away at the presence of the Lord, like wax before the fire, * the whole earth too has trembled at his presence.

The heavens have declared his righteousness, * and all the people have beheld his glory.

May they all be confounded, who adore graven things : * and who glory in their idols.

Adore him, all ye his

Angeli ejus: * audivit et lætáta est Sion.

Et exultavérunt filiæ Judæ, * propter judícia tua, Dómine:

Quóniam tu Dóminus altíssimus super omnem terram: * nimis exaltátus es super omnes deos.

Qui dilígitis Dóminum, odíte malum: * custódit Dóminus ánimas sanctórum suórum, de manu peccatóris liberábit eos.

Lux orta est justo, * et rectis corde lætítia.

Lætámini justi in Dómino: * et confitémini memóriæ sanctificatiónis ejus.

Glória Patri, &c.

Antiphona. Dignàri me laudáre te, Virgo sacrata: da mihi virtútem contra hostes tuos.

angels: * Sion hath heard his voice, and was filled with gladness.

And the daughters of Juda have rejoiced,* on account of thy judgments, O Lord.

Because thou, O Lord, art most high above all the earth: * thou art exceedingly exalted above all gods.

All you, who love the Lord, detest evil; * the Lord watcheth over the souls of his saints, and will deliver them from the power of sinners.

Light is risen for the just, * and joy for the upright of heart.

Ye just, rejoice in the Lord, * and render glory to the author of all sanctity.

Glory be to the Father, &c.

Anthem. Vouchsafe that I may praise thee, O sacred virgin, obtain for me strength against my enemies.

(*Per annum*) *Antiphona.* Post partum.

(*In Adventu*) *Antiphona.* Angelus Dómini.

Psalmus xcvii.

CANTATE Dómino cánticum novum; * quia mirabília fecit.

Salvávit sibi déxtera ejus; * et bráchium sanctum ejus.

Notam fecit Dóminus salutáre suum : * in conspéctu Géntium revelávit justitiam suam.

Recordátus est misericórdiæ suæ, * et veritátis suæ dómui Israël.

Vidérunt omnes términi terræ * salutare Dei nostri.

Jubiláte Deo omnis terra : * cantàte, et exultáte, et psállite.

Psàllite Dómino in

(*Through the year*) *Anth.* After thy childbirth.

(*In Advent*) *Anth.* The Angel of the Lord.

Psalm 97.

SING to the Lord a new canticle : * because he has wrought many wonderful things.

His strong hand has effected salvation, * and also his divine power.

The Lord hath made known the promised Saviour :* he hath revealed his righteousness before the nations.

He hath been mindful of his mercy, * and of the inviolable promises he made to Israel.

All the boundaries of the earth have beheld * the salvation, which our God has wrought.

Let the whole earth praise God with joy, * may it chaunt forth, and rejoice, and sing canticles to him.

Sing praises to the

cíthara, in cíthara et voce psalmi : * in tubis ductílibus, et voce tubæ córneæ.

Lord on the harp, with the melody of the psalter : * on the metal trumpet, accompanied with the music of the cornet.

Jubiláte in conspectu Regis Dómini : * moveátur mare, et plenitúdo ejus ; orbis terrárum, et qui hábitant in eo.

Make joyful harmony before the Lord, our king : * may the sea, and all its fulness, may the earth, and its inhabitants, be moved to exultation.

Flúmina plaudent manu, simul montes exultábunt á conspéctu Dómini : * quóniam venit judicáre terram.

The rivers shall applaud, the mountains too shall rejoice before the Lord : * for he cometh to judge the earth.

Judicábit orbem terrárum in justítia, * et pópulos in æquitáte.

He will judge the world with justice, * and all the people according to the truth of his holy law.

Glória Patri, &c.

Glory be to the Father, &c.

(Per annum) Antiphona. Post partum virgo invioláta permansísti, Dei génetrix, intercéde pro nobis.

(Through the year) Anthem. After thy child-birth thou didst remain an inviolate virgin, O mother of God, make intercession for us.

(In Adventu) Anti-

(In Advent) Anthem.

phona. Angelus Dómini nunciávit Maríæ, et concépit de Spíritu Sancto, allelúia.

V. Diffúsa est grátia in lábiis tuis. *R.* Proptéreá benedixit te Deus in ætérnum.

Pater noster. *Secreto.*

V. Et ne nos indúcas in tentatiónem. *R.* Sed líbera nos á malo.

Absolutio.

Precibus et méritis beátæ Maríæ semper víginis et ómnium Sanctorum, perdúcat nos Dóminus ad regna cœlórum. *R.* Amen.

V. Jube, domne benedícere.

Benedictio. Nos cum Prole pia benedícat virgo María. *R.* Amen.

The angel of the Lord declared unto Mary, and she conceived by the Holy Ghost, alleluia.

V. Grace is spread on thy lips. *R.* Therefore God hath blessed thee for ever.

Our Father. In *silence.*

V. And lead us not into temptation. *R.* But deliver us from evil.

Absolution.

By the prayers and merits of the ever blessed Virgin Mary, and of all the saints, may the Lord bring us to the kingdom of heaven. *R.* Amen.

V. Pray, father, give me your blessing.

The Blessing. May the Virgin Mary obtain for us the blessing of her divine son. *R.* Amen.

(*These following Lessons are said throughout the year, except during Advent.*)

Lectio i. *Eccli.* xxiv.

In ómnibus réquiem quæsívi, et in hereditáte Dómini morábor. Tunc

The first Lesson. Ecc. 24.

I sought every where for a place of rest, and I shall dwell in the in-

præcépit et dixit mihi Creátor ómnium: et qui creavit me requiévit in tabernáculo meo, et dixit mihi: In Jacob inhábita, et in Israël hereditáre, et in eléctis meis mitte radíces. Tu autem, Domine, miserére nobis. *R.* Deo gratias.

R. Sancta et immaculáta virgínitas, quibis te láudibus éfferam néscio: * Quia quem cœli cápere non póterant, tuo grémio contulísti.

V. Benedícta tu in muliéribus, et benedíctus fructus ventris tui. *R.* Quia quem cœli capere non póterant tuo grémio contulísti.

V. Jube domine benedícere.
Benedictio. Ipsa Virgo

heritance of the Lord. Then the Creator of the universe hath given me orders, and spoke unto me: He, who has created me, reposed in my tabernacle, and said to me: Let thy dwelling be in Jacob, and thy inheritance in Israel, and take root among my elect. But, thou, O Lord, have mercy on us. *R.* Thanks be to God.

R. O holy and immaculate virginity, I know not with what praises to extol thy dignity: * Because whom the heavens could not contain, thou hast borne in thy womb.

V. Blessed art thou among women, and blessed is the fruit of thy womb. *R.* Because whom the heavens could not contain, thou hast borne in thy womb.

V. Pray, father, give me your blessing.
The Blessing. May

MATINS.

vírginum intercédat pro nobis ad Dóminum.

Lectio ii.

Et sic in Sion firmàta sum, et in civitáte sanctificáta, simíliter requiévi, et in Jerúsalem potéstas mea. Et radicavi in pópulo honorificáto, et in parte Dei mei heréditas illíus, et in plenitudine sanctórum deténtio mea. Tu autem, Dómine, miserére nobis. *R.* Deo grátias.

R. Beáta es virgo María, quæ Dóminum portásti, Creatórem mundi : * Genuísti qui te fecit, et in æternum pérmanes virgo.

V. Ave María, grátia plena : Dóminus tecum. *R.* Genuísti qui te fecit, et in æternum pérmanes Virgo.

the Virgin of virgins make intercession for us to the Lord.

The second Lesson.

I have likewise dwelt in Sion, and have rested in the holy city, and my power was strengthened in Jerusalem. I settled myself among a people, whom the Lord hath honoured, and hath chosen for his portion and inheritance, and have fixed my abode in the company of all the saints. But thou, O Lord, have mercy on us. *R.* Thanks be to God.

R. Blessed art thou, O Virgin Mary, who has borne the Lord, and Creator of the world : * Thou hast brought forth him, who made thee, and remainest ever a virgin.

V. Hail, Mary, full of grace, the Lord is with thee. *R.* Thou hast brought forth him, who made thee, and remainest ever a Virgin.

When the Hymn, Te Deum, *is said, after the third Lesson, the last verse of this Responsory is again repeated, thus:*

Glória Patri, et Fílio, et Spirítu Sancto. *R.* Genuísti qui te fecit, et in ætérnum pérmanes virgo.	Glory be to the Father, and to the Son, and to the Holy Ghost. *R.* Thou hast brought forth him, who made thee, and remainest ever a Virgin.
V. Jube, domine, benedícere.	*V.* Pray, father, give me your blessing.
Benedictio. Per vírginem matrem concédat nobis Dominus salútem et pacem. *R.* Amen.	*The Blessing.* May the Lord, through the intercession of the Virgin Mother, grant us salvation and peace. *R.* Amen.

Lectio iii.

The third Lesson.

Quasi cedrus exaltáta sum in Libanon, et quasi cypréssus in monte Sion: quasi palma exaltáta sum in Cades, et quasi plantátio rosæ in Jericho: quasi olíva speciósa in campis, et quasi plátanus exaltáta sum juxta aquam in platéis. Sicut cinnamónum et bálsamum aromatízans odórem de-

I am exalted like the cedar on Libanon, and as the cypress-tree on Mount Sion: I have grown like the plane-tree in Cades, and as the rose-plant in Jericho: I have flourished like a fair olive-tree in the fields, and as a palm-tree watered by the stream. I yielded forth a fragrant smell like

di : quasi myrrha elécta dedi suavitátem odóris. Tu autem, Dómine, miserére nobis. R. Deo gratias.

cinnamon and aromatic balm : and, like the best myrrh, I spread around the sweetest odour. But thou, O Lord, have mercy on us. R. Thanks be to God.

The following Responsory is omitted, when the Hymn Te Deum *is said.*

R. Felix namque es sacra virgo María, et omni laude digníssima : * Quia ex te ortus est Sol justítiæ, * Christus, Deus noster.

R. Thou art truly happy, O sacred Virgin Mary, and most worthy of all praise : * Because out of thee is risen the Sun of righteousness,* Jesus Christ, our God.

V. Ora pro pópulo, intérveni pro clero, intercéde pro devóto fœmíneo sexu : séntiant omnes tuum juvamen, quicúmque célebrant tuam sanctam commemoratiónem. R. Quia ex te ortus est Sol justítiæ.

V. Pray for the people, intercede for the clergy, plead for the devout female sex; let all be sensible of thy aid, who celebrate thy holy memory. R. Because of thee is risen the Sun of righteousness.

Glória Patri et Fílio, et Spirítu Sancto. R. Christus, Deus noster.

Glory be to the Father, and to the Son, and to the Holy Ghost. R. Jesus Christ, our God.

The following Hymn may be said from the

solemnity of Christmas to the Saturday before Septuagesima Sunday, and from the solemnity of Easter to the Saturday before the first Sunday of Advent.

When it is said, the Responsory of the third Lesson is omitted, and to the second Responsory the Glory be to the Father *is added, and the last versicle repeated, as above marked. This Hymn is not said in Advent, and from Septuagesima Sunday to Easter Saturday, except on the occurring Feasts of the Blessed Virgin Mary, viz:* The Conception, 8th of December; the Expectation, 18th do.; the Annunciation, 25th of March; the seven Dolours, Friday in Passion Week, and the Purification, 2nd of February, when it falls on or after Septuagesima Sunday.

Hymnus SS. Ambrosii et Augustini.	*Hymn of St. Ambrose and St. Augustine.*
Te Deum, laudámus: te Dóminum confitémur.	Thee, sov'reign God, our grateful accents praise; We own thee, Lord, and bless thy wondrous ways.
Te æternum Patrem, omnis terra venerátur.	To thee, eternal Father, earth's whole frame, With loudest trumpets sounds immortal fame;
Tibi, omnes Angeli: tibi cœli, et univérsæ potestátes.	Lord, God of Hosts! for thee the heav'nly pow'rs With sounding anthems fill the vaulted tow'rs;

MATINS. 73

Tibi Chèrubim et Seraphim, incessábili voce proclámant,	Thy Cherubim, thy Seraphim, thrice holy cry,
Sanctus, Sanctus, Sanctus, Dóminus Deus Sábaoth.	To thee, O God, who dwells and reigns on high.
Pleni sunt cœli et terra, majestátis glóriæ tuæ.	Both heav'n and earth thy majesty display,
	They owe their beauty to thy glorious ray.
Te gloriósus Apostolórum chorus,	Thy praises fill the loud apostles' choir,
Te Prophetárum laudábilis númerus,	The train of prophets in the song conspire.
Te Mártyrum candidátus laudat exércitus,	Red hosts of martyrs in the chorus shine,
	And vocal blood with vocal music join.
Te per orbem terrárum sancta confitétur Ecclésia,	By these thy Church inspir'd with heav'nly art,
	Around the world maintains a second part;
Patrem imménsæ majestátis,	And tunes her sweetest notes, O God, for thee,
	The Father of unbounded majesty,
Venerándum tuum verum, et únicum Fílium,	The Son, ador'd Co-partner of thy seat,
Sanctum quoque Paráclitum Spiritum.	And equal everlasting Paraclete.

Tu Rex glóriæ Christe,	Thou King of glory, Christ of the Most High,
Tu Patris sempitérnus es Fílius;	Thou co-eternal filial Deity;
Tu, ad liberándum susceptúrus hóminem, non horruísti Vírginis úterum.	Thou, who to save the world's impending doom, Vouchsaf'st to dwell within a virgin's womb.
Tu devicto mortis acúleo, aperuísti credéntibus regna cœlórum	Old tyrant Death disarm'd, before thee flew, The bolts of heav'n, and back the foldings drew,
Tu ad déxteram Dei sedes, in glória Patris.	To give access, and make the faithful way, From God's right hand thy filial beams display,
Judex créderis esse ventúrus.	Thou art to judge the living and the dead;
Te ergo, quæsumus, tuis fámulis súbveni, quos pretióso sánguine redemísti.	Then spare those souls for whom thy veins have bled.

At this last verse all should make a genuflection

Ætérna fac cum sánctis tuis in glória numerári.	O take us up amongst the blest above, To share with them in thy eternal love.

MATINS.

Salvum fac pópulum tuum, Dómine, et bénedic hereditáti tuæ.	Preserve, O Lord, thy people, and enhance Thy blessing on thy own inheritance.
Et rege eos, et extólle illos usque in ætérnum.	For ever raise their hearts, and rule their ways,
Per síngulos dies benedícimus te:	Each day we bless thee, and proclaim thy praise.
Et laudámus nomen tuum in sæculum, et in sæculum sæculi.	No age shall fail to celebrate thy name, Nor hour neglect thy everlasting fame
Dignáre, Dómine, die isto, sine peccáto nos custodíre.	Preserve our souls, O Lord, this day from ill:
Miserére nostri, Dómine: miserére nostri.	Have mercy on us, Lord, have mercy still.
Fiat misericórdia tua, Dómine, super nos, quemádmodum sperávimus in te.	As we have hoped, do thou reward our pain:
In te, Dómine, sperávi, non confúndar in ætérnum.	We've hop'd in thee, let not our hope be vain.

The Lauds immediately follow, which are set down after the Lessons of Advent, p. 81.

In Advent.

After the Psalms of the Nocturn, according to the order of the day, the following Prayers and Lessons are said:—

Pater noster, &c. secreto.	Our Father, &c., *in silence.*

V. Et ne nos indúcas in tentatiónem. *R.* Sed líbera nos à malo.

Absolutio.

PRECIBUS et méritis beátæ Maríæ semper Vírginis, et ómnium sanctórum, perdúcat nos Dóminus ad regna cœlórum. *R.* Amen.

V. Jube, domine, benedícere.

Benedictio. Nos cum Prole pia benedícat virgo María. *R.* Amen.

Lectio i. *Lucæ* 1.

MISSUS est ángelus Gábriel à Deo in civitátem Galilææ, cui nomen Názareth, ad vírginem desponsátam viro, cui nomen erat Joseph, de domo David; et nomen vírginis María. Et ingréssus ángelus ad eam, dixit: Ave, grátia plena: Dóminus tecum : benedícta tu in muliéribus. Tu autem Dómine, mi-

V. And lead us not into temptation. *R.* But deliver us from evil.

Absolution.

BY the prayers and merits of the ever blessed Virgin Mary, and of all the saints, may the Lord bring us to the kingdom of heaven. *R.* Amen.

V. Pray, father, give me your blessing.

The Blessing. May the Virgin Mary obtain for us the blessing of her divine Son. *R.* Amen.

The first Lesson. Luke 1.

THE angel Gabriel was sent by God to a city of Galilee, called Nazareth, to a virgin espoused to a man whose name was Joseph, of the house of David: and the virgin's name was Mary. And the angel having entered, said unto her: Hail, full of grace, the Lord is with thee: blessed art thou

serére nobis. *R.* Deo grátias.

R. Missus est Gábriel ángelus ad Maríam vírginem desponsátam Joseph, núntians ei verbum : et expavéscit virgo de lúmine. Ne tímeas María, invenísti grátiam apud Dóminum : * Ecce concípies, et paries, et vocábitur Altíssimi Filius.

V. Dabit ei Dóminus Deus sedem David, patris ejus, et regnábit in domo Jacob in æternum. *R.* Ecce concípies, et páries, et vocábitur Altíssimi Filius.

V. Jube domine, benedícere.
Benedictio. IpsaVirgo

among women. But thou, O Lord, have mercy on us. *R.* Thanks be to God.

R. The angel Gabriel was sent to the Virgin Mary, espoused to Joseph, to announce to her the divine message : but the light of his countenance affrighted the sacred Virgin. Do not fear, Mary, thou hast found grace with the Lord : * Behold, thou shalt conceive, and bring forth a Son, who shall be called the Son of the Most High.

V. The Lord God shall give him the throne of his father David, and he shall eternally reign over the house of Jacob. *R.* Behold, thou shalt conceive, and bring forth a Son, who shall be called the Son of the Most High.

V. Pray, father, give me your blessing.
Blessing. May the

Lectio ii.

Quæ cùm audisset, turbáta est in sermóne ejus, et cogitábat qualis esset ista salutátio. Et ait Angelus ei: Ne tímeas María, invenísti enim grátiam apud Deum: ecce, concípies in útero, et páries fílium, et vocábis nomen ejus Jesum. Hic erit magnus Fílius Altíssimi vocábitur: et dabit illi Dóminus Deus sedem David patris ejus, et regnábit in domo Jacob in ætérnum, et regni ejus non erit finis. Tu autem, Dómine, miserére nobis. *R.* Deo grátias.

R. Ave, María, grátia plena: Dóminus tecum. * Spíritus Sanctus

The second Lesson.

Mary having heard these words, was much troubled, and reflected on what kind of salutation this could be. And the angel said to her: Do not fear, Mary, for thou hast found grace with God: behold, thou shalt conceive in thy womb, and shalt bring forth a Son, and shalt call his name Jesus. He shall be great, and shall be called the Son of the Most High: the Lord God will give him the throne of his father David, and he shall eternally reign over the house of Jacob, and of his kingdom there shall be no end. But thou, O Lord, have mercy on us. *R.* Thanks be to God.

R. Hail, Mary, full of grace: the Lord is with thee. * The Holy

supervéniet in te, et virtus Altíssimi obumbrábit tibi: quod enim ex te nascétur Sanctum, vocàbitur Fílius Dei.

V. Quómodo fiet istud, quóniam virum non cognósco? Et respondens Angelus, dixit ei. *R.* Spíritus Sanctus supervéniet in te, et virtus Altíssimi obumbrábit tibi: quod enim ex te nascétur Sanctum, vocábitur Fílium Dei.

V. Jube, domine, benedicere.
Benedictio. Per Vírginem matrem concédat nobis Dóminus salútem et pacem. *R.* Amen.

Lectio iii.

Dixit autem María ad Angelum: Quómodo fiet istud, quóniam virum non cognósco? Et respóndens Angelus,

Ghost shall descend on thee, and the virtue of the Most High shall overshadow thee: for the Holy One, who will be born of thee, shall be called the Son of God.

V. How shall this be done, because I know not man? The angel answering, said to her: *R.* The Holy Ghost shall descend on thee, and the virtue of the Most High shall overshadow thee: for the Holy One, who will be born of thee, shall be called the Son of God.

V. Pray, father, give me your blessing.
Blessing. May the Lord, through the intercession of the virgin mother, grant us salvation and peace. *R.* Amen.

The third Lesson.

Then Mary said to the angel: How shall this be done, for I know not man? The angel answered her:

dixit ei : Spíritus Sanctus supervéniet in te, et virtus Altíssimi obumbrábit tibi. Ideóque et quod nascétur ex te Sanctum vocábitur Fílius Dei. Et ecce Elízabeth, cognáta tua, et ipsa concépit fílium in senectúte sua : et hic mensis sextus est illi, quæ vocátur stérilis : quia non erit impossibile apud Deum omne verbum. Dixit autem María : Ecce ancilla Dómini, fiat mihi secúndum verbum tuum. Tu autem, Dómine, miserére nobis. *R*. Deo grátias.

R. Súscipe verbum, Virgo María, quod tibi à Dómino per Angelum transmíssum est : concípies, et páries Deum pàriter et hóminum : * Ut benedícta dicáris inter omnes mulíeres.

The Holy Ghost shall descend on thee, and the virtue of the Most High shall overshadow thee : therefore the Holy One, who will be born of thee, shall be called the Son of God. And behold, thy cousin Elizabeth hath conceived a son in her old age ; and this month is the sixth to her, who is called barren ; for with God nothing shall be impossible. Mary then replied : Behold the handmaid of the Lord, be it done to me according to thy word. But thou, O Lord, have mercy on us. *R*. Thanks be to God.

R. Receive, O Virgin Mary, the word which the Lord declared to thee by the ministry of the angel : thou shalt conceive, and bring forth a Son, who will be both God and man : * That thou mayest be called blessed among all women.

V. Páries quidem fílium, et virginitátis non patièris detrimentum; efficiéris grávida, et eris mater semper intácta. *R.* Ut benedícta dicáris inter omnes mulíeres.

Glória Patri, et Fílio, et Spirítui Sancto. *R.* Ut benedícta dicáris inter omnes mulíeres.

V. Thou shalt bring forth a Son, and shalt suffer no detriment in thy virginity: thou shalt become a mother, without ceasing to be a chaste virgin. *R.* That thou mayest be called blessed among all women.

V. Glory be to the Father, and to the Son, and to the Holy Ghost. *R.* That thou mayest be called blessed among all women.

On the feasts of the blessed Virgin Mary, the 8th and 18th of December, the above Hymn of Thanksgiving may be said: the last Responsory is omitted, the Glory be to the Father *is added to the second Responsory, and the last Versicle is again repeated.*

AT LAUDS.

Ave, María, &c.
V. Deus, in adjutórium meum inténde. *R.* Dómine, ad adjuvándum me festína.
Glória Patri, &c.

(*Per annum*) *Anti-*

Hail Mary, &c.
V. Incline unto my aid, O God. *R.* O Lord, make haste to help me.
Glory be to the Father, &c.

(*Through the year*)

phona. Assúmpta est María.

(*In Adventu*) *Antiphona.* Missus est Gàbriel ángelus.

(*Tempore Nativ.*) *Antiphona.* O admirábile commércium!

Psalmus xcii.

Dominus regnávit, decórum indútus est; * indútus est Dóminus fortitúdinem, et præcínxit se.

Etenim firmávit orbem terræ, * qui non commovébitur.

Paráta sedes tua ex tunc: * á sæculo tu es.

Elevavérunt flúmina, Dómine: * elevavérunt flúmina vocem suam.

Elevavérunt flumina fluctus suos: * á vócibus aquárum multárum.

Miràbiles elatiónes maris,* mirábilis in altis Dóminus.

Anthem. Mary is taken up.

(*In Advent*) *Anthem.* The angel Gabriel was sent.

(*Christmas time*) *Antiphona.* O admirable intercourse!

Psalm 92.

The Lord hath reigned, and is clothed with beauty; * he is covered with strength, and well girded.

For he hath founded the earth on its basis, * which shall not be disturbed.

Thy throne was prepared before the world: * thou art from eternity.

The floods have risen O Lord: * the floods have roared aloud.

The rivers have swelled their waves: * their roaring is the noise of many waters.

Wonderful are the surges of the sea: * but more wonderful is the Lord, who rules over all things.

LAUDS. 83

Testimonia tua credibília facta sunt nimis: * domum tuam decet sanctitúdo, Dómine, in longitudinem diérum.

Glória Patri, &c.

(*Per annum*) *Antiphona.* Assúmpta est María in cœlum, gaudent Angeli, laudantes benedicunt Dóminum.

Antiph. María Virgo.

(*In Adventu*) *Anthem.* Missus est Gábriel ángelus ad Maríam vírginem, desponsàtam Joseph.

Antiph. Ave, María.

(*Tempore Nativ.*) *Antiphona.* O admirábile commércium! Creátor géneris humáni, animátum corpus sumens, de Vírgine nasci dignátus est: et procédens homo sine sémine, largítus est nobis suam Deitátem.

Thy testimonies are become exceedingly credible: * holiness becometh thy house, O Lord, unto length of days.

Glory be to the Father, &c.

(*Through the year*) *Anthem.* Mary is taken up into heaven; the angels rejoice in her glory, and with praises bless the Lord.

Anth. The Virgin Mary.

(*In Advent*) *Anthem.* The angel Gabriel was sent to the Virgin Mary, espoused to Joseph.

Anth. Hail Mary.

(*Christmas time*) *Anthem.* O wonderful intercourse! the Creator of mankind, assuming a body animated with a soul, was pleased to be born of a virgin: and becoming man, without human concurrence, he made us partakers of his divine nature.

Antiph. Quando natus es.

Psalmus xcix.

Jubilate Deo omnis terra; * servíte Dómino in lætítia.

Introíte in conspéctu ejus, * in exultatióne.

Scitóte quóniam Dóminus ipse est Deus : * ipse fecit nos, et non ipsi nos.

Pópulus ejus, et oves páscuæ ejus; * introíte portas ejus in confessióne, átria ejus in hymnis : confitémini illi.

Laudáte nomen ejus : quóniam suávis est Dóminus, in æternum misericórdia ejus, * et usque in generatiónem et generatiónem véritas ejus.

Glória Patri, &c.

(*Per annum*) *Antiphona.* María virgo as-

Anth. When thou wast born.

Psalm 99.

Sing joyfully to the Lord ye people of the earth : * serve the Lord with delight of heart.

Present yourselves before him * in transports of holy joy.

Know ye, that the Lord himself is the only God : * he hath made us, and not we ourselves.

We are his people, and the sheep of his pasture : * enter into the porches of his temple, singing his divine praises, and giving him glory.

Praise ye his name : for the Lord is sweet; his mercies are eternal, * and his truth endureth from generation to generation.

Glory be to the Father, &c.

(*Through the year*) *Anthem.* The Virgin

súmpta est ad æthéreum thálamum, in quo Rex regum stelláto sedet sólio.

Antiph. In odórem unguentórum.

(*In Adventu*) *Antiphona.* Ave, María, grátia plena, Dóminus tecum : benedícta tu in muliéribus.

Antiph. Ne tímeas, María.

(*Tempore Nativ.*) *Antiphona.* Quando natus es ineffabíliter ex Vírgine, tunc implétæ sunt Scriptúræ: sicut plúvia in vellus descendísti, ut salvum fáceres genus humánum : te laudámus, Deus noster.

Antiph. Rubum quem víderat Móyses.

Psalmus lxii.

Deus, Deus meus,* ad te de luce vígilo.

Sítivit in te ánima

Mary is taken up into the heavenly chamber, where the King of kings sits on his throne, brilliant with stars.

Anth. We run after the odour.

(*In Advent*) *Anthem.* Hail, Mary, full of grace, the Lord is with thee : blessed art thou among women.

Anthem. Fear not, Mary.

(*Christmas time*) *Anthem.* When thou wast born after an ineffable manner, the Scriptures were then fulfilled; thou didst descend like rain upon a fleece, to save mankind : O our God, we give thee praise.

Anth. In the bush, which Moses saw.

Psalm 62.

O God, my God, * I watch unto thee from the dawn of the day.

My soul hath thirsted

mea, * quám multiplíciter tibi caro mea!

In terra desérta, et ínvia, et inaquósa: * sic in sancto appárui tibi: ut viderem virtútem tuam, et gloriam tuam.

Quóniam mélior est misericórdia tua super vitas: * lábia mea laudábunt te.

Sic benedícam te in vita mea: * et in nómine tuo levábo manus meas.

Sicut ádipe et pinguédine repleátur ánima mea: * et lábiis exultatiónis laudábit os meum.

Si memor fui tui super stratum meum, in matutínis meditábor in te: * quia fuísti adjútor meus.

Et in velaménto alà-

after thee; * oh, by how many titles doth my whole being belong to thee!

In this desert, uncultivated, and barren land, * I shall be in thy presence, as if I were in the sanctuary, to contemplate thy power and thy glory.

For thy mercies are preferable to many lives: * my lips shall not cease to praise thee.

Thus I will bless thee all my life: * and I will lift up my hands to praise thy name.

May my soul be replenished with thy benedictions, as with the fatness of marrow: * and my mouth shall praise thee with rapturous joy.

I have called thee to mind on my bed at night, and in the morning I will meditate on thee; * because thou hast been my helper.

Under the covert of

LAUDS.

rum tuárum exultábo; adhæsit ánima mea post te: * me suscépit déxtera tua.

Ipsi veró in vanum quæsiérunt ánimam meam; introíbunt in inferióra terræ : * tradéntur in manus gládii, partes vúlpium erunt.

Rex vero lætábitur in Deo, laudabúntur omnes qui jurant in eo: * quia obstrùctum est os loquéntium iníqua.

thy wings I will rejoice; my soul is attached to thee: * thy right hand hath protected me.

And my enemies have in vain sought my soul, they shall descend into the lower regions of the earth: * unto the justice of the sword they shall be delivered, and shall become a prey to ravenous foxes.

But the king shall rejoice in God: all, who swear by him, shall be glorified; * because he hath stopt the mouths of those, who speak evil things.

The Glory be to the Father, &c. *is not said here.*

Psalmus lxvi.   Psalm 66.

Deus misereátur nostri, et benedícat nobis: * illúminet vultum suum super nos, et misereátur nostri.

Ut cognoscámus in terra viam tuam, * in ómnibus géntibus salutáre tuum.

May God have mercy on us, and bless us: * may he regard us with a favourable countenance, and have mercy on us.

May we know thy ways on earth, * and may all nations seek thy salvation.

Confiteántur tibi pópuli, Deus : * confiteántur tibi pópuli omnes.

Læténtur et exultent gentes : quóniam júdicas pópulos in æquitáte, et gentes in terra dírigis.

Confiteántur tibi pópuli Deus : confiteántur tibi pópuli omnes : * terra dedit fructum suum.

Benedicat nos Deus, Deus noster, benedícat nos Deus : * et métuant eum omnes fines terræ.

Gloria Patri, &c.

(*Per annum*) *Antiphona.* In odórem unguentórum tuórum cúrrimus : adolescéntulæ dilexérunt te nimis.

Antiph. Benedicta, fília, tu.

(*In Adventu*) *Antiphona.* Ne tímeas,

May the people confess to thee, O God : * may all present to thee their praises.

Let the nations be glad, and rejoice : for thou dost judge the people with equity, and rulest over all the nations of the earth.

May the people confess thee, O God : may all present to thee their praises : * the earth hath yielded forth her fruit.

May the Lord, our God, bless us, may he give us his blessing : * and may all the bounds of the earth fear him.

Glóry be to the Father, &c.

(*Through the year*) *Anthem.* We run after the odour of thy perfumes : the young virgins have exceedingly loved thee.

Anth. Thou art blessed O daughter.

(*In Advent*) *Anthem.* Do not fear, Mary, thou

María, invenísti grátiam apud Dóminum: ecce concípies, et páries Fílium.

Antiph. Dabit ei Dóminus.

(Tempore Nativ.) Antiphona. Rubum, quem víderat Móyses incombùstum, conservátam agnóvimus tuam laudábilem virginitátem: Dei génetrix, intercéde pro nobis.

Antiph. Germinávit radix Jesse.

Canticum trium Puerorum. Dan. iii.

BENEDÍCITE, ómnia ópera Dómini, Dómino: * laudáte et superexaltáte eum in sæcula.

Benedícite, ángeli Dómini, Dómino: * benedícite cœli Dómino.

Benedícite, aquæ omnes quæ super cœlos sunt Dómino: * bene-

hast found grace with the Lord: behold, thou shalt conceive, and bring forth a Son.

Anth. The Lord will give.

(Christmas time) Anthem. In the bush, which Moses saw burning without consuming, we acknowledge the preservation of thy admirable virginity: O mother of God, make intercession for us.

Anth. The root of Jesse hath buddeth forth.

Canticle of the three Children. Dan. 3.

ALL ye works of the Lord, bless the Lord: * praise and extol him for ever.

Bless the Lord, ye angels of the Lord: * ye heavens, bless the Lord.

All ye waters, which lie suspended on the firmament, bless the

dícite ómnes virtútes Dómini, Dómino.

Benedícite, sol et luna Dómino ; * benedícite, stellæ cœli, Dómino.

Benedícite, omnis imber et ros, Dómino : * benedícite, omnes spíritus Dei Dómino.

Benedícite, ignis et æstus, Dómino : * benedícite, frigus et æstus, Dómino.

Bendícite, rores et pruina, Dómino : benedícite, gelu et frigus, Dómino.

Bendícite, glácies et nives, Dómino : benedícite, noctes et dies, Dómino.

Bendícite, lux et ténebræ, Dómino : * benedícite, fúlgura et nubes, Dómino.

Benedícat terra Dóminum : * laudet et superexáltet eum in sæcula.

Benedícite, montes et colles, Dómino : * bene-

Lord : * bless the Lord, all ye powers of the Lord.

Sun and moon, bless the Lord : * stars of the firmament, bless the Lord.

Every shower and dew, bless the Lord : * all ye tempestuous winds, bless the Lord.

Fire and heat, bless the Lord : * cold and heat, bless the Lord.

Dews and hoar-frosts, bless the Lord ; frost and cold, bless the Lord.

Ice and snow, bless the Lord : nights and days, bless the Lord.

Light and darkness, bless the Lord : * lightnings and clouds, bless the Lord.

May the earth bless the Lord ; * may it praise and extol him for ever.

Mountains and hills bless the Lord : * herbs,

dícite, univérsa germinántia in terra, Dómino.

Benedícite, fontes, Dómino : * benedícite, mária et flúmina, Dómino.

Benedícite, cete, et ómnia, quæ moventur in aquis, Dómino : * benedícite, omnes volúcres cœli, Domino.

Benedícite, omnes béstiæ et pécora, Dómino : * benedícite, fílii hóminum, Dómino.

Benedícat Israël Dóminum ; * laudet et superexáltet eum in secula.

Benedícite, sacerdótes Dómini, Dómino : * benedícite, servi Dómini, Dómino.

Benedícite, spíritus et ánimæ justorum, Dómino : * benedícite, sancti et húmiles corde, Dómino.

Benedícite, Anania, Azaría, Misael, Dómino ; * laudàte et superexaltáte eum in sæcula.

Benedícamus Patrem et Fílium cum Sancto

and plants, bless the Lord.

Ye fountains, bless the Lord : * seas and rivers, bless the Lord.

Whales, and all ye creatures which live in the waters, bless the Lord : * all ye birds of the air, bless the Lord.

All beasts and cattle, bless the Lord : * ye children of men, bless the Lord.

May Israel bless the Lord : * may he praise and extol him for ever.

Ye priests of the Lord, bless the Lord : * ye servants of the Lord, bless the Lord.

Spirits and souls of the just, bless the Lord : * ye holy and humble of heart, bless the Lord.

O Ananias, Azarias, Misael, bless ye the Lord ; * praise and extol him for ever.

Let us bless the Father, and the Son, with

Spíritu ; * laudémus et superexaltémus eum in sæcula.

Benedíctus es, Dómine, in firmaménto cœli : * et laudábilis, et gloriósus, et superexaltàtus in sæcula.

the Holy Ghost ; * let us praise and glorify him for ever.

Blessed art thou, O Lord, in the firmament of heaven : * to thee be rendered all praise, honour, and glory, for ever.

The Glory be to the Father, &c. *is not said here.*

(*Per annum*) *Antiphona.* Benedícta fília tu á Dómino, quia per te fructum vitæ communicávimus.

(*Through the year*) *Anthem.* Thou art blessed by the Lord, O daughter, for through thee we have been made partakers of the fruit of life.

Antiph. Pulchra es, et decóra.

Anth. Thou art fair and beautiful.

(*In Adventu*) *Antiphona.* Dabit ei Dóminus sedem David, patris ejus, et regnábit in æternum.

(*In Advent*) *Anthem.* The Lord will give him the throne of David, his father, and he shall reign for ever.

Antiph. Ecce ancílla Dómini.

Anth. Behold the handmaid of the Lord.

(*Tempore Nativ.*) *Antiphona.* Germinávit radix Jesse : orta est stella ex Jacob ; virgo péperit Salvatórem : te laudámus, Deus noster.

(*Christmas time*) *Anthem.* The root of Jesse hath budded forth: a star hath arisen out of Jacob : a virgin hath brought forth the Saviour : we give thee praise, O our God.

Antiph. Ecce María génuit.

Psalmus cxlviii.

LAUDATE Dóminum de cœlis : * laudate eum in excélsis.

Laudáte eum, omnes ángeli ejus : * laudáte eum, omnes virtútes ejus.

Laudáte eum, sol et luna : * laudáte eum, omnes stellæ et lumen.

Laudáte eum, cœli cœlórum : * et aquæ omnes, quæ super cœlos sunt, laudent nomen Dómini.

Quia ipse dixit, et facta sunt : * ipse mandávit, et creáta sunt.

Státuit ea in ætérnum, et in sæculum sæculi : * præcéptum pósuit, et non præteríbit.

Laudáte Dóminum

Anth. Behold Mary hath borne.

Psalm 148.

PRAISE the Lord in the heavens : * praise him in the highest places.

Praise him, all ye his angels : * praise him, ye celestial powers.

Praise him, sun and moon : * praise him, all ye stars and light.

Praise him, O heaven of heavens ! * and may the waters, that are over the firmament, praise the name of the Lord.

For he hath spoken the word, and all things were made : * he hath commanded, and they were created.

He hath established his works for length of ages : * he prescribed to them his wise regulations, which shall not be transgressed.

Praise the Lord, from

de terra, * dracónes, et omnes abyssi.

Ignis, grando, nix, glácies, spíritus procellárum : * quæ fáciunt verbum ejus.

Montes, et omnes colles : * ligna fructífera, et omnes cedri.

Béstiæ, et univérsa pecora : * serpéntes, et volúcres pennátæ :

Reges terræ, et omnes pópuli : * príncipes, et omnes júdices terræ.

Júvenes, et vírgines : senes cum junióribus laudent nomen Dómini : * quia exaltátum est nomen ejus solíus.

Conféssio ejus super cœlum et terram : * et exaltávit cornu pópuli sui.

Hymnus ómnibus sanctis ejus : * fílius Israël, pópulo appropinquánti sibi.

the earth, * ye dragons, and all ye depths.

Fire, hail, snow, ice, and stormy winds : * which obey his orders :

Mountains, and all hills : * fruit-bearing trees, and all cedars.

Beasts, and herds of cattle : * reptiles and birds of the air.

Kings of the earth, and all ye people : * princes, and judges of the earth,

Young men and maidens : the old with the young, let them praise the name of the Lord : * for his name alone is most worthy of all praise.

His praise is above heaven and earth, * and he hath exalted the power of his people.

May hymns of praise be rendered to him by all his saints : * by the children of Israel, his cherished people.

The Glory be to the Father, *&c. is not said here.*

LAUDS.

Psalmus cxlix.

CANTATE Dómino cánticum novum; * laus ejus in ecclésia sanctórum.

Lætétur Israël in eo, qui fecit eum : * et fílii Sion exúltent in rege suo.

Laudent nomen ejus in choro : * in tympano et psaltério psallant ei.

Quia beneplácitum est Dómino in pópulo suo : * et exaltábit mansuétos in salútem.

Exultábunt sancti in glória : * lætabúntur in cubílibus suis.

Exaltatiónes Dei in gútture eórum : * et gládii ancípites in mánibus eórum,

Ad faciéndam vindictam in natiónibus, * increpatiónes in pópulis,

Ad alligándos reges

Psalm 149.

SING to the Lord a new canticle : may his praises resound in the assembly of the saints.

May Israel rejoice in the God who made him : * may the sons of Sion exult in their king.

May they celebrate his name in choir : * and honour him by concert on the timbrel and the psaltery.

For the Lord is well pleased with his people : * and he will exalt the meek unto salvation.

The saints in glory shall be filled with joy : * they shall rejoice on their couches.

Sublime praises of God are in their mouths : * and two-edged swords in their hands,

To execute vengeance on the nations, * and chastisement on the people,

To bind their kings

eórum in compédibus, * et nóbiles eórum in mánicis férreis.

Ut fáciant in eis judícium conscríptum : * glória hæc est ómnibus sanctis ejus.

in fetters, * and their nobles with iron manacles.

They shall thus exercise the decreed justice : * this glory is reserved for all his saints.

The Glory be to the Father, &c. *is not said here.*

Psalmus cl.

Psalm 150.

Laudate Dóminum in sanctis ejus : * laudáte eum in firmaménto virtútis ejus.

Laudáte eum in virtútibus ejus : * laudáte eum secúndùm multitúdinem magnitúdinis ejus.

Laudáte eum in sono tubæ : * laudáte eum in psaltério, et cíthera.

Laudáte eum in tympano, et choro : * laudáte eum in chordis, et órgano.

Laudáte eum in cymbalis benesonántibus : laudáte eum in cymbalis jubilatiónis : * omnis

Praise the Lord in his sanctuary : * praise him in the firmament of his power.

Praise him in his mighty deeds : * praise him according to his exceeding greatness.

Praise him with the sound of trumpet : * praise him on the psaltery and the harp.

Praise him on the timbrel and in choir : * praise him on stringed instruments, and on the organ.

Praise him with the best sounding cymbals, praise him on instruments of jubilee : * may

spíritus laudet Dominum.

Glória Patri, &c.

(*Per annum*) *Antiphona.* Pulchra es, et decóra, fília Jerúsalem, terríbilis ut castrórum ácies ordináta.

(*In Adventu*) *Antiphona.* Ecce ancílla Dómini, fiat mihi secúndùm verbum tuum.

(*Tempore Nativ.*) *Antiphona.* Ecce María génuit nobis Salvatórem, quem Joánnes videns, exclamávit, dicens : Ecce, agnus Dei, ecce, qui tollit peccáta mundi, alleluia.

every living creature praise the Lord.

Glory be to the Father, &c.

(*Through the year*) *Anthem.* Thou art fair and beautiful, O daughter of Jerusalem, formidable as an army in battle array.

(*In Advent*) *Anthem.* Behold the hand-maid of the Lord, be it done unto me according to thy word.

(*Christmas time*) *Anthem.* Behold, Mary hath born to us the Saviour, whom John seeing, cried out: Behold the lamb of God, behold him, who taketh away the sins of the world, alleluia.

(*The Little Chapter through the year, except in Advent.*)

Capitulum. Cant. vi.

Viderunt eam, fíliæ Sion, et beatíssimam prædicavérunt, et regínæ laudavérunt eam. *R.* Deo grátias.

Little Chapter. Cant. 6.

The daughters of Sion beheld her, and declared her most blessed, and queens have highly praised her. *R.* Thanks be to God.

(*In Advent.*)

Capitulum. Isaiæ xi.

Egredietur virga de radíce Jesse, et flos de radíce ejus ascendet : et requiéscet super eum Spíritus Dómini. *R.* Deo grátias.

Little Chapter. Isa. 11.

There shall spring forth a branch out of the root of Jesse, and a flower shall arise out of its stock : and the Spirit of the Lord shall rest upon him. *R.* Thanks be to God.

Hymnus.

O gloriosa Vírginum,

Sublímis inter sídera,

Qui te creávit, párvulum
Lacténte nutris úbere.

Quod Heva tristis ábstulit,
Tu reddis almo gérmine:

Intrent ut astra flébiles,

Cœli reclúdis cárdines.

Tu regis alti jánua,

Et aula lucis fúlgida :

Vitam datam per Vírginem,

Hymn.

O Mary ! whilst thy Maker blest

Is nourish'd at thy virgin breast,

Such glory shines, that stars, though bright,
Compar'd to thee, all lose their light.

The loss that man in Eve deplores
Thy fruitful womb in Christ restores,

And makes the way to heaven free

For those, who mourning follow thee.

By thee the heav'nly gates display,

And shew the light of endless day :

Sing ransom'd nations, sing and own,

Gentes redémptæ pláudite.
Jesu, tibi sit glória,

Qui natus es de Vírgine,

Cum Patre et almo Spíritu,
In sempitérna sæcula. Amen.

V. Benedícta tu in muliéribus, R. Et benedíctus fructus ventris tui.

(*Per annum*) *Antiphona.* Beáta Dei génitrix María.

(*Tempore paschali*) *Antiphona.* Regína cœli.

(*In Adventu*) *Antiphona.* Spíritus Sanctus.

(*Tempore Nativ.*) *Antiphona.* Mirábile mysterium.

Canticum Zachariæ, Lucæ i.

BENEDICTUS Dóminus, Deus Israël : * quia visitávit, et fecit redemptiónem plebis suæ :

Your ransom was a Virgin's Son.
To thee, O Jesus, Mary's Son,

Be everlasting homage done,

To God the Father, we repeat
The same, and to the Paraclete. Amen.

V. Blessed art thou among women. R. And blessed is the fruit of thy womb.

(*Through the year*) *Anthem.* O blessed Mary, mother of God.

(*In Easter time*) *Anthem.* O queen of heaven.

(*In Advent*) *Anthem.* The Holy Ghost.

(*Christmas time*) *Anthem.* A wonderful mystery.

Canticle of Zachary, Luke 1.

BLESSED be the Lord, the God of Israel : * because he hath visited, and effected the redemption of his people.

Et eréxit cornu salútis nobis, * in domo David, púeri sui.

Sicut locútus est per os sanctórum, * qui à sæculo sunt, prophetárum ejus:

Salútem ex inimícis nostris, * et de manu ómnium qui odérunt nos:

Ad faciéndam misericórdiam cum pátribus nostris; * et memorári testaménti sui sancti.

Jusjurándum, quod jurávit ad Abraham patrem nostrum, * datúrum se nobis,

Ut sine timóre, de manu inimicórum nostrórum liberáti, * serviámus illi,

In sanctitáte et justítia coram ipso, * ómnibus diebus nostris.

Et tu, puer, prophéta Altíssimi vocáberis: * præíbis enim ante fá-

And he hath raised up a powferful Saviour for us,* in the house of David, his servant.

As he promised by the mouth of his holy prophets,* from the beginning:

To save us from our enemies,* and from the hands of all who hate us:

To communicate his mercy to us, as well as to our Fathers; * and to recal to mind the holy covenant, made to them.

The oath, which he hath sworn to our father Abraham, * that he would grant us the grace,

That, being rescued from the fear and power of our enemies, * we may serve him,

In holiness and righteousness in his presence, * all the days of our lives.

And thou, O happy child, shalt be called the prophet of the Most

ciem Dómini paráre vias ejus:

Ad dandam sciéntiam salútis plebi ejus, * in remissiónem peccatórum eórum.

Per víscera misericórdiæ Dei nostri: * in quibus visitávit nos, óriens ex alto:

Illumináre his, qui in ténebris, et in umbra mortis sedent: * ad dirigéndos pedes nostros in viam pacis.

Gloria Patri, &c.

(*Per annum*) *Antiphona.* Beáta Dei génetrix María, virgo perpetua, templum Dómini, sacrárium Spíritus Sancti, sola sine exemplo placuísti Dómino nostro, Jesu Christo: ora pro pópulo, interveni pro clero, intercéde pro devóto fœmíneo sexu.

High: * for thou shalt go before the face of the Lord to prepare his ways:

To give his people the knowledge of salvation* unto the remission of their sins.

Through the bowels of the mercy of our God : * with which he, like the rising sun from on high, hath visited us.

To give light to those who sit in darkness, and in the shade of death : * to guide our feet into the ways of peace.

Glory be to the Father, &c.

(*Through the year*) *Anthem.* O blessed Mary, mother of God, and ever virgin, temple of the Lord, and sanctuary of the Holy Ghost, thou alone didst please our Lord, Jesus Christ, in a most singular and perfect manner; pray for the people, plead for the clergy, and intercede for the devout female sex.

(Tempore paschali) Antiphona. Regína cœli lætáre, allelúia, quia quem meruísti portáre, allelúia, resurrexit sicut dixit, allelúia: ora pro nobis Deum, allelúia.

(In Adventu) Antiphona. Spíritus Sanctus in te descéndet, María: ne tímeas, habébis in útero Fílium Dei, allelúia.

(Tempore Nativ.) Antiphona. Mirábile mystérium declarátur hódie: innovántur naturæ: Deus homo factus est: id, quod fuit, permánsit: quod non erat, assúmpsit: non commixtiónem passus, neque divisiónem.

Kyrie eleíson. Kyrie eleíson. Kyrie eleíson.

V. Dómine, exáudi oratiónem meam. *R.* Et clamor meus, ad te véniat.

(Easter time) Anthem. O queen of heaven, rejoice, alleluia, because he, whom thou didst deserve to bear, alleluia, is risen again, as he foretold, alleluia: pray for us to God, alleluia.

(In Advent) Anthem. The Holy Ghost shall come upon thee Mary: do not fear, thou shalt have in thy womb the Son of God, alleluia.

(Christmas time) Anthem. A most sublime mystery is made manifest on this day; wonders are wrought in nature: God is made man: still remaining what he was: he assumed what he was not: he suffered no mixture, nor division.

Lord, have mercy on us. Christ, have mercy on us. Lord, have mercy on us.

V. O Lord, hear my prayer. *R.* And let my cry come unto thee.

LAUDS. 103

Or, if the president be a priest or a deacon.

V. Dóminus vobíscum. R. Et cum Spíritu tuo.

Oremus.

V. The Lord be with you. R. And with thy Spirit.

Let us pray.

(*The prayer through the year, except at Christmas time.*)

Deus, qui beátæ Maríæ vírginis útero Verbum tuum, Angelo nunciánte, carnem suscípere voluísti; præsta súpplicibus tuis, ut qui verè eam genitrícem Dei crédimus, ejus apud intercessionibus adjuvémur. Per eúndem Christum Dóminum nostrum. R. Amen.

O God, who wast pleased that thy eternal word, when the angel delivered his message, should take flesh in the womb of the blessed Virgin Mary: give ear to our humble petitions, and grant that we, who believe her to be truly the mother of God, may be assisted by her prayers. Through the same Christ, our Lord. Amen.

(*Tempore Nativ.*)— Deus, qui salútis ætérnæ beátæ Maríæ virginitáte fœcúnda humáno géneri præmia præstitísti: tríbue, quæsumus, ut ipsam pro nobis intercédere sentiámus, per quam meruímus auctórem vitæ suscípere, Dóminum nostrum, Je-

(*Christmas time*). O God, who, by the fruitful virginity of blessed Mary, hast given to mankind the rewards of eternal salvation, grant, we beseech thee, that we may experience her intercession for us, by whom we deserved to receive the author of

sum Christum, Fílium tuum. *R.* Amen.

life, our Lord Jesus Christ, thy Son. *R.* Amen.

Commemoration of the Saints.
(*Through the year, except in Advent.*)

Antiphona. Sancti Dei omnes intercédere dignémini pro nostra omniúmque salúte.

Anthem. All ye saints of God, vouchsafe to make intercession for the salvation of us, and of all mankind.

V. Lætámini in Dómino, exultáte, justi. *R.* Et gloriámini, omnes recti corde.

V. Rejoice in the Lord, ye just, and be exceedingly glad. *R.* And exult in glory, all ye upright of heart.

Oremus.

Let us pray.

Protege, Dómine, pópulum tuum, et apostolórum tuorum Petri et Pauli, et aliórum Apostolórum patrocínio confidentem, perpétua defensióne consérva.

Protect, O Lord, thy people, and grant us thy continual assistance, which we humbly beg with confidence, through the intercession of St. Peter and St. Paul, and of thy other apostles.

Omnes Sancti tui, quæsumus, Dómine, nos ubíque ádjuvent; ut dum eórum mérita recólimus, patrocínia sentiámus: et pacem tuam nostris concéde tempóribus, et ab Ecclésia tua

May all thy saints, we beseech thee, O Lord, always assist our weakness, that whilst we celebrate their merits we may experience their protection; grant us thy peace in our days, and

cunctam repélle nequítiam : iter actus, et voluntátes nostras, et ómnium famulórum tuórum, in salútis tuæ prosperitáte dispóne: benefactóribus nostris sempitérna bona retríbue, et ómnibus fidélibus defúnctis réquiem ætérnum concéde. Per Dóminum nostrum, Jesum Christum, Fílium tuum, qui tecum vivit et regnat in unitáte Spíritus Sancti, Deus, per ómnia sæcula sæculórum. R. Amen.

banish all evils from thy Church : prosperously guide the steps, actions, and desires of us, and of all thy servants, in the way of salvation : give eternal blessings to our benefactors, and grant everlasting rest to all the faithful departed. Through our Lord, Jesus Christ, thy Son, who liveth and reigneth with thee, and the Holy Ghost, one God, world without end. R. Amen.

(*Commemoration of the Saints in Advent.*)

Antiphona. Ecce Dóminus, véniet, et omnes sancti ejus cum eo: et erit in die illa lux magna, allelúia.

Anthem. Behold, the Lord will come, and all his saints with him : and there shall be a great light on that day, alleluia.

V. Ecce, apparébit Dóminus in nubem cándidam. R. Et cum eo sanctórum míllia.

V. Behold, the Lord shall appear on a bright cloud. R. And with him thousands of saints.

Orenius.

Let us pray.

Conscientias nostras, quæsumus, Dómi-

Visit and purify our consciences, O Lord,

he, visitando purifica, ut véniens Jesus Christus, Fílius tuus, Dóminus noster, cum ómnibus sanctis, parátam sibi in nobis invéniat mansiónem: Qui tecum vivit et regnat in unitáte Spíritus Sancti, Deus, per omnia sæcula sæculórum. *R.* Amen.

that Jesus Christ, thy Son, our Lord, coming with all his saints, may find in us an abode prepared for his reception: who liveth and reigneth with thee, and the Holy Ghost, one God, world without end. *R.* Amen.

After the commemoration for the Saints, the following Versicles are said.

V Dómine exáudi oratiónem meam. *R.* Et clamor meus ad te veniat.

V. O Lord, hear my prayer. *R.* And let my cry come unto thee.

V. Benedicámus Dómino. *R.* Deo grátias.

V. Let us bless the Lord. *R.* Thanks be to God.

V. Fidélium ánimæ per misericórdiam Dei requiéscant in pace. *R.* Amen.

V. May the souls of the faithful departed, through the mercy of God, rest in peace. *R.* Amen.

Pater noster, &c. *Secreto.*

Our Father, &c *In silence.*

V. Dóminus det nobis suam pacem. *R.* Et vitam ætérnam. Amen.

V. May the Lord grant us his peace. *R.* And life everlasting. Amen.

Then is recited one of the Anthems of the

Blessed Virgin Mary, according to the time of the year, as above, p. 36, and the following pages: after the prayer, is said this Versicle, which terminates Lauds.

V. Divínum auxílium máneat semper nobíscum. *R.* Amen.

V. May the divine assistance always remain with us. *R.* Amen.

The prayer after Office, May all praise, &c. *p. 5, is said kneeling.*

Note.—*If the lesser Hours, or any of them, be immediately said after Lauds, the above Lord's Prayer and Anthem are not said here, but after the Versicle,* May the souls of the fathful, &c., *the following hour of Prime begins: at the end of the last canonical hour, the* Lord's Prayer *and Anthem, as remarked, are recited: then the Prayer after Office.*

AT PRIME.

O DIVINE and adorable Lord Jesus Christ, who hast graciously redeemed us by thy bitter passion and death, we offer up this hour of Prime to thy honor and glory, and most humbly beseech thee, through the great humility thou didst undergo, in being convicted before the false tribunals of Pilate and Herod, where thou wast reviled by the soldiery, clothed like a fool, and degraded below the worst of criminals, to grant us true humility of heart, and sincere sentiments of our own wretchedness, misery, poverty, blindness and destitution, that we may never esteem ourselves above the lowest of our fellow-creatures, but always acknowledge ourselves truly the worst of sinners, so that our extreme misery may excite thy tender compassion and infinite goodness to forgive us all our sins, to replenish us with thy divine grace here, and to elevate us to eternal glory in heaven. Amen.

Ave, Maria, &c.   Hail Mary, &c.

V. Deus, in adjutóriam meum inténde. *R.* Dómine, ad adjuvàndum me festína.

Gloria Patri, &c.

Hymnus.

Memento, rerum Cónditor,

Nostri quód olim córporis,

Sacráta ab alvo Vírginis

Nascéndo, formam sumpseris.

Maria, mater grátiæ,

Dulcis parens cleméntiæ,

Tu nos ab hoste prótege,

Et mortis hora súscipe.

Jesu, tibi sit glória,

Qui natus es de Vírgine,

Cum Patre et almo Spíritu,

In sempitérna sæcula. Amen.

(*Per annum*) Anti-

V. Incline unto my aid, O God *R.* O Lord make haste to help me.

Glory be to the Father, &c.

Hymn.

Remember thou, Creator Lord,

The Father, God's co-equal Word,

To save mankind, from virgin's womb

Our human nature didst assume.

O Happy Mary full of grace,

Dear mother of the prince of peace,

Protect us from our evil foe,

And bliss at death on us bestow.

To thee, O Jesus, Mary's Son,

Be everlasting homage done,

To God the Father we repeat

The same, and to the Paraclete. Amen.

(*Through the year*)

phona. Assúmpta est María.

(*In Adventu*). *Antiphona.* Missus est Gábriel ángelus.

(*Tempore Nativ.*) *Antiphona.* O admirábile commércium!

Psalmus liii.

Deus in nómine tuo salvum me fac : * et in virtúte tua júdica me.

Deus exáudi oratiónem meam : * áuribus percipe verba oris mei.

Quóniam aliéni insurrexérunt advérsum me, et fortes quæsiérunt ánimam meam : * et non proposuérunt Deum ante conspéctum suum.

Ecce enim Deus adjuvat me : * et Dóminus suscéptor est ánimæ meæ.

Avérte mala inimícis meis : * et in veritáte tua dispérde illos.

Anthem. Mary is taken up.

(*In Advent*) *Anthem.* The angel Gabriel was sent.

(*Christmas time*) *Anthem.* O admirable intercourse!

Psalm 53.

Save me, O God, in thy name : * and in thy power do me justice.

O God, graciously hear my prayer : * give ear to my words.

For strangers have risen up against me, and strong ones have sought to take away my soul : * and they have not been mindful of the presence of God.

For behold, God is my helper : * and the Lord is the protector of my soul.

Turn back on my enemies the evils, which they wish to do me : * and destroy them according to the truth of thy words.

Voluntárie sacrificábo tibi, * et confitébor nomini tuo, Dómine: quóniam bonum est:

Quoniam ex omni tribulatióne eripuísti me: * et super inimícos meos despéxit óculus meus.

Glória Patri, &c.

Psalmus lxxxiv.

BENEDIXISTI, Dómine terram tuam: * avertísti captivitátem Jacob.

Remisísti iniquitátem plebis tuæ: * operuísti ómnia peccáta eórum.

Mitigásti omnem iram tuam: * avertísti ab ira indignatiónis tuæ.

Convérte nos, Deus, salutáris noster: * et avérte iram tuam á nobis.

Numquid in ætérnum irascéris nobis? * aut exténdes iram tuam á generatióne in generatiónem?

I will freely sacrifice to thee,* and will praise thy holy name, O Lord: because it is just:

For thou hast rescued me from all trouble; * and I have regarded my enemies without fear.

Glory be to the Father, &c.

Psalm 84.

O LORD, thou hast blessed thy land: * thou hast set free the captives of Jacob.

Thou hast forgiven the iniquity of thy people: * thou hast pardoned all their sins.

Thou hast mitigated all thy anger: * and withdrawn from us thy indignation

Convert us to thee, O God, our Saviour: * and turn away thy wrath from us.

Wilt thou be for ever angry with us? * or wilt thou continue thy wrath from generation to generation?

Deus, tu convérsus vivificábis nos : * et plebs tua lætábitur in te.

Osténde nobis, Dómine, misericórdiam tuam, * et salutáre tuum da nobis.

Audiam quid loquátur in me Dóminus Deus : * quóniam loquétur pacem in plebem suam :

Et super sanctos suos, * et in eos, qui convertúntur ad cor.

Verúmtamen propé timéntes eum salutáre ipsíus; * ut inhábitet glória in terra nostra.

Misericórdia et véritas obviavérunt sibi : * justitia et pax osculátæ sunt.

Véritas de terra orta est : * et justítia de cœlo prospéxit.

Etenim Dóminus dabit benignitátem : * et

O God, thou wilt cheer us with thy reconciliation : * and thy people shall rejoice in thee.

Shew us, O Lord, thy mercy, * and grant us thy salvation.

I will hear what the Lord God will speak in me : * for he will speak peace unto his people :

He will announce it to his saints, * and to those, whose heart is truly converted to him.

Surely his salvation is near to those, who fear him; * that his glory may dwell among us.

Mercy and truth have met each other : * justice and peace have kissed.

Truth is sprung out of the earth : * and justice hath regarded us from the height of heaven.

For the Lord will communicate his good-

terra nostra dabit fructum suum.

Justítia ante eum ambulábit : * et ponet in via gressus suos.

Glória Patri, &c.

Psalmus cxvi.

Laudate Dóminum, omnes gentes: * laudáte eum, omnes pópuli.

Quóniam confirmáta est super nos misericórdia ejus : * et véritas Dómini manet in æternum.

Glória Patri, &c.

(*Per annum*) *Antiphona.* Assúmpta est María in cœlum : gaudent Angeli, laudántes, benedícunt Dóminum.

(*In Adventu*) *Antiphona.* Missus est Gábriel ángelus ad Maríam vírginem, desponsátam Joseph.

(*Tempore Nativ.*)*Antiphona.* O admirábile

ness : * and the earth shall yield her fruit.

Justice shall proceed before him : * and shall direct his steps in the true path.

Glory be to the Father, &c.

Psalm 116.

Praise the Lord, all ye nations : * praise him, all ye people.

For his mercy is confirmed upon us : * and the truth of the Lord remaineth for ever.

Glory be to the Father, &c.

(*Through the year*) *Anthem.* Mary is taken up into heaven : the angels rejoice, and with praises bless the Lord.

(*In Advent*) *Anthem.* The angel Gabriel was sent to the virgin Mary, espoused to Joseph.

(*Christmas time*) *Anthem.* O wonderful in-

commércium! Creátor géneris humáni animátum corpus sumens de vírgine nasci dignátus est: et procédens homo sine sémine, largitus est nobis suam Deitátem.

tercourse! the Creator of mankind, assuming a body animated with a soul, was pleased to be born of a virgin; and becoming man without human concurrence, made us partakers of his divine nature.

(*The Little Chapter through the year, except in Advent.*)

Capitulum. Cant. vi.

Quæ est ista, quæ progréditur quasi Auróra consúrgens, pulchra ut luna, elécta ut sol, terríbilis ut castrórum ácies ordináta? *R.* Deo grátias.

Little Chapter. Cant. 6.

Who is she, that cometh forth as the morning rising, beautiful like the moon, bright as the sun, formidable as an army in battle array? *R.* Thanks be to God.

(*In Advent.*)

Capitulum. Isai. vii.

Ecce virgo concípiet, et páriet fílium, et vocábitur nomen ejus Emmánuel. Butyrum et mel cómedet, ut sciat reprobare malum, et elígere bonum. *R.* Deo grátias.

Little Chapter. Isaias 7.

Behold, a virgin shall conceive, and bring forth a son, and his name shall be called Emmanuel. He shall eat butter and honey, that he may know how to reject evil, and choose good. *R.* Thanks be to God.

V. Dignáre me lau-

V. Vouchsafe, O sa-

dáre te, Virgo sacràta. *R.* Da mihi virtútem contra hostes tuos.

Kyrie eleison. Christe eleison. Kyrie eleison.

V. Dómine exáudi oratiónem meam. *R.* Et clamor meus ad te véniat.

Oremus.

(*Per annum*) Deus, qui virginálem aulam beatæ Maríæ, in qua habitáres, elígere dignatus es; da, quæsumus, ut sua nos defensióne munitos, jucúndos fácias suæ interésse commemoratióni: Qui vivis et regnas cum Deo Patre in unitáte Spíritus Sancti, Deus, per ómnia sæcula sæculorum. *R.* Amen.

(*In Adventu*) Deus, qui de beátæ Maríæ Vírginis útero Verbum

cred Virgin, to accept of my praises. *R.* Give me strength against thy enemies.

Lord, have mercy on us. Christ, have mercy on us. Lord, have mercy, on us.

V. O Lord, hear my prayer. *R.* And let my cry come unto thee.

Let us Pray.

(*Through the year*) O God, who wast pleased to make choice of the chaste womb of the blessed Virgin Mary for thy abode; grant, we beseech thee, that being protected by the assistance of her intercession, we may celebrate her memory with spiritual joy: Who livest and reignest with the Father and the Holy Ghost, one God, world without end. *R.* Amen.

(*In Advent*) O God, who wast pleased that thy eternal word, when

tuum, Angelo nuntiánte, carnem suscípere voluísti; præsta supplícibus tuis, ut qui verè eam genitrícem Dei crédimus, ejus apud te intercessiónibus adjuvémur. Per eúmdem Dóminum nostrum, Jesum Christum, Fílium tuum, qui tecum vivit et regnat in unitáte Spíritus Sancti, Deus, per ómnia sæcula sæculórum. *R.* Amen.

(*Tempore Nativ.*) Deus, qui salútis ætérnæ, beátæ Maríæ virginitáte fœcúnda, humáno géneri præmia præstitísti; tríbue, quæsumus, ut ipsam pro nobis intercédere sentiámus, per quam merúimus auctórem vitæ suscípere; Dóminum nostrum, Jesum Christum, Fílium tuum : Qui tecum vivit et regnat in unitáte Spíritus Sancti, Deus, per ómnia sæcula sæculórum. *R.* Amen.

the angel delivered his message, should take flesh in the womb of the blessed Virgin Mary; give ear to our humble petitions, and grant that we, who believe her to be truly the mother of God, may be assisted by her prayers. Through the same Lord Jesus Christ, thy son, who liveth and reigneth with thee and the Holy Ghost, one God, world without end. *R.* Amen.

(*Christmas time*) O God, who by the fruitful virginity of blessed Mary, hast given to mankind the rewards of eternal salvation; grant, we beseech thee, that we may experience her intercession, by whom we have received the author of life, our Lord Jesus Christ, thy Son: Who liveth and reigneth with thee and the Holy Ghost, one God, world without end. *R.* Amen.

V. Dómine, exáudi oratiónem meam. *R.* Et clamor meus ad te véniat.	*V.* O Lord, hear my prayer. *R.* And let my cry come unto thee.
V. Benidicàmus Dómino. *R.* Deo grátias.	*V.* Let us bless the Lord. *R.* Thanks be to God.
V. Fidélium ànimæ per misericórdiam Dei, requiéscant in pace. *R.* Amen.	*V.* May the souls of the faithful departed, through the mercy of God, rest in peace. *R.* Amen.

AT TERCE.

O DIVINE and adorable Lord, Jesus Christ, who hast graciously redeemed us by thy bitter passion and death, we offer up this hour of Terce to thy honour and glory; and most humbly beseech thee, through the torments thou didst endure in being cruelly scourged at a pillar, crowned with thorns, and unjustly condemned to be crucified, to grant us patience and longanimity under the scourges of temporal afflictions, courage to walk in the thorny road to the narrow gate, which opens to bliss, and perseverance under all the crosses of this life, which are the portion of the elect, that by suffering for our sins, we may fully satisfy thy divine justice on earth, and may enter into thy glory immediately after death. Amen.

Ave María, &c.	Hail, Mary, &c.
V. Deus, in adjutórium meum inténde. *R.* Dómine, ad adjuvándum me festína.	*V.* Incline unto my aid, O God. R. O Lord, make haste to help me.
Glória Patri, &c.	Glory be to the Father, &c.
Hymnus.	*Hymn.*
MEMENTO, rerum, &c.	REMEMBER thou, &c.

(*Per annum*) *Antiphona.* María virgo.

(*In Adventu*) *Antiphona.* Ave, María.

(*Tempore Nativ.*) *Antiph.* Quando natus es.

Psalmus cxix.

Ad Dóminum cum tribulárer clamávi, * et exaudívit me.

Dómine, líbera ánimam meam á lábiis iníquis, * et á linguo dolósa.

Quid detur tibi, aut quid appónatur tibi, * ad linguam dolósam?

Sagíttæ poténtis acutæ, * cum carbónibus desolatóriis.

Heu mihi, quia incolátus meus prolongátus est! habitávi cum habitántibus Cedar: * multum íncola fuit anima mea.

(*Through the year*) *Anthem.* The Virgin Mary.

(*In Advent*) *Anthem.* Hail, Mary.

(*Christmas time*) *Anthem.* When thou wast born.

Psalm 119.

I cried out to the Lord in my extreme distress, * and he graciously heard me.

O Lord, deliver my soul from unjust lips, * and from a deceitful tongue.

What shall be done to thee, or what punishment shalt thou receive * for thy deceitful tongue?

Thou shalt feel the sharp arrows of the mighty, * accompanied with destructive burning coals.

How miserable I am, that my exile is so prolonged! I dwell here among the inhabitants of Cedar: * my soul hath been long a sojourner.

Cum his, qui odérunt pacem, eram pacíficus: * cum loquébar illis impugnábant me gratis.

Glória Patri, &c.

Psalmus cxx.

Levavi óculos meos in montes: * unde véniet auxílium mihi.

Auxílium meum á Dómino, * qui fecit coelum et terram.

Non det in commotiónem pedem tuum: * neque dormítet, qui custódit te.

Ecce non dormitábit, neque dórmiet, * qui custódit Israël.

Dóminus custódit te, Dóminus protéctio tua, * super manum déxteram tuam.

Per diem sol non uret te, * neque luna per noctem.

Dóminus custódit te ab omni malo: * cus-

I was peaceable with those, who hated peace: * when I spoke to them, they opposed me without any cause.

Glory be to the Father, &c.

Psalm 120.

I lifted up my eyes towards the mountains: * from whence I expect assistance.

My help is from the Lord, * who made heaven and earth.

May he not suffer thy foot to be moved: * neither may he slumber, who is thy guardian.

Behold, he shall neither slumber nor sleep,* that keepeth Israel.

The Lord watcheth over thee, the Lord is thy protector: * he is at thy right hand.

The sun shall not burn thee by day, * nor shall the moon molest thee by night.

The Lord preserveth thee from all evil: *

TERCE.

tódiat ánimam tuam Dóminus.

Dóminus custódiat intróitum tuum, et éxitum tuum, * ex hoc nunc, et usque in sæculum.

Glória Patri, &c.

Psalmus cxxi.

Lætatus sum in his, quæ dicta sunt mihi: * in domum Dómini íbimus.

Stantes erant pedes nostri * in átriis tuis, Jerúsalem.

Jerúsalem, quæ ædificátur ut cívitas, * cujus participátio ejus in idípsum.

Illuc enim ascendérunt tribus, tribus Domini; * testimónium Israël ad confiténdem nómini Dómini.

Quia illic sedérunt sedes in judício, * sedes super domum David.

Rogáte quæ ad pacem sunt Jerùsalem; *

may the Lord still protect thy soul.

May the Lord watch over thee coming in, and going out, * now and for evermore.

Glory be to the Father, &c.

Psalm 121.

I rejoiced in what hath been told me: * we are to go up to the house of the Lord.

Our feet have stood * in thy courts, O Jerusalem.

Jerusalem, which is now building like a city, * all whose parts are well combined.

For thither the tribes went up, the tribes of the Lord; * according to the ordinances given to Israel to praise the name of the Lord.

For there were placed the judgment-seats, * the judgment-seats over the house of David.

Pray for whatever maketh for the peace of

et abundántia diligéntibus te.

Fiat pax in virtúte tua : * et abundàntia in túrribus tuis.

Propter fratres meos et próximos meos, * loquébar pacem de te.

Propter domum Dómini, Dei nostri, * quæsívi bona tibi.

Glória Patri, &c.

(*Per annum*) *Antiphona.* María Virgo assúmpta est ad æthéreum thálamum, in quo Rex regum stelláto sedet sólio.

(*In Adventu*) *Antiphona.* Ave, María, grátia plena, Dóminus tecum; benedícta tu in muliéribus.

(*Tempore Nativ.*) *Antiphona.* Quando natus es ineffabíliter ex Vírgine, tunc implétæ sunt Scriptúræ: sicut plúvia in vellus descen-

Jerusalem; * and may plenty be to all, who love thee.

May peace be in thy strength: * and plenty within thy walls.

For the sake of my brethren and of my neighbours, * I have advocated thy peace.

For the sake of the house of the Lord, our God, * I have sought good things for thee.

Glory be to the Father, &c.

(*Through the year*) *Anthem.* The Virgin Mary is taken up into the heavenly chamber, where the King of kings sits on his starry throne.

(*In Advent*) *Anthem.* Hail, Mary, full of grace, the Lord is with thee; blessed art thou among women.

(*Christmas time*) *Anthem.* When thou wast born after an ineffable manner, the Scriptures were then fulfilled: thou didst descend like rain

dísti, ut salvum fáceres genus humánum: te laudámus, Deus noster.

upon a fleece, to save mankind: O our God, we give thee praise.

(*Little Chapter through the year, except in Advent.*)

Capitulum. Eccl. xxiv.

Little Chapter. Ec. 24.

Et sic in Sion firmáta sum, et in civitáte sanctificáta simíliter requiévi, et in Jerúsalem potéstas mea. *R.* Deo grátias.

And so was I established in Sion, and in the holy city likewise I rested, and my power was in Jerusalem. *R.* Thanks be to God.

(*In Advent.*)

Capitulum. Isaiæ xi.

Little Chapter. Isa. 11.

Egredietur virga de radíce Jesse, et flos de radíce ejus ascéndet. Et requiéscet super eum Spíritus Dómini. *R.* Deo grátias.

There shall spring forth a branch out of the root of Jesse, and a flower shall arise out of its stock: and the spirit of the Lord shall rest upon him. *R.* Thanks be to God.

V. Diffúsa est grátia in lábiis tuis. *R.* Proptéreà benedíxit te Deus in ætérnum.

V. Grace is spread on thy lips. *R.* Therefore God hath blessed thee for ever.

Kyrie eleíson. Christe eleíson. Kyrie eleíson.

Lord, have mercy on us. Christ, have mercy on us. Lord, have mercy on us.

V. Dómine, exáudi

V. O Lord, hear my

orationem meam. *R.* Et clamor meus ad te véniat.

Oremus.

prayer. *R.* And let my cry come unto thee.

Let us pray.

(*The Prayer through the year, except in Advent.*)

Deus, qui salútis ætérnæ, beátæ Maríæ vírginitáte fœcúnda, humáno géneri præmia præstitísti, tríbue, quæsumus; ut ipsam pro nobis intercédere sentiámus, per quam merúimus auctórem vitæ suscípere, Dóminum nostrum, Jesum Christum, Fílium tuum: Qui tecum vivit et regnat in unitáte Spíritus Sancti, Deus, per ómnia sæcula sæculórum. *R.* Amen.

O God, who by the fruitful virginity of blessed Mary, hast given to mankind the rewards of eternal salvation; grant, we beseech thee, that we may experience her intercession for us, by whom we deserved to receive the author of life, our Lord, Jesus Christ, thy Son, who liveth and reigneth with thee and the Holy Ghost, one God, world without end. Amen.

Oremus.

Let us pray.

(*In Adventu*) Deus, qui de beátæ Maríæ vírginis útero Verbum tuum, Angelo nunciánte, carnem suscípere voluísti; præsta supplícibus tuis, ut qui verè eam genitrícem Dei crédimus, ejus apud te intercessiónibus adjuvé-

(*In Advent*) O God, who wast pleased that thy eternal word, when the angel delivered his message, should take flesh in the womb of the blessed Virgin Mary: give ear to our humble petitions, and grant that we, who believe her to

mur. Per eúndem Dóminum nostrum, Jesum Christum, &c.

V. Dómine, exáudi oratiónem meam. *R.* Et clamor meus ad te véniat.

V. Benedicámus Domino. *R.* Deo grátias.

V. Fidélium ánimæ, per misericórdiam Dei, requiéscant in pace. *R.* Amen.

be truly the Mother of God, may be helped by her prayers. Through the same Lord, Jesus Christ, &c.

V. O Lord, hear my prayer. *R.* And let my cry come unto thee.

V. Let us bless the Lord. *R.* Thanks be to God.

V. May the souls of the faithful departed, through the mercy of God, rest in peace. *R.* Amen.

AT SEXT.

O DIVINE and adorable Lord, Jesus Christ, who hast graciously redeemed us by thy bitter passion and death, we offer up this hour of Sext to thy honour and glory; and most humbly beseech thee, through the faintings thou didst experience in bearing the cross from Pilate's tribunal to Calvary, and the excessive pains thou didst suffer when thy tender hands and feet were cruelly pierced through with gross nails, and fastened to the cross, to grant us thy strengthening grace to arise immediately whenever we fall into sin, and to restrain our hands, our feet, and our other sensitive powers from injuring our neighbour, and from evil deeds, that we may rise up, and go to our celestial Father with our hands replete with good works, to merit thy eternal rewards. Amen.

Ave, María, &c.   Hail, Mary, &c.

V. Deus, in adjutórium meum inténde. *R.* Dómine, ad adjuvándum me festína.

Glória Patri, &c.
Hymnus.

Memento, rérum, &c.

(*Per annum*) *Antiphona.* In odórem unguentórum.

(*In Adventu*) *Antiphona.* Ne tímeas, María.

(*Tempore Nativ.*) *Antiphona.* Rubum, quem víderat Móyses.

Psalmus cxxii.

Ad levávi óculos meos, * qui hábitas in cœlis.

Ecce sicut óculi servórum * in mánibus dominorum suórum:

Sicut óculi ancíllæ in mánibus dóminæ suæ: * ita óculi nostri ad Dóminum, Deum nostrum, donec misereátur nostri.

Misérere nostrî, Dó-

V. Incline unto my aid, O God. *R.* O Lord, make haste to help me.

Glory, &c.
Hymn.

Remember thou, &c.

(*Through the year*) *Anthem.* We run after the odour.

(*In Advent*) *Anthem.* Do not fear, Mary.

(*Christmas time*) *Anthem.* In the bush, which Moyses saw.

Psalm 122.

To thee have I lifted up my eyes, * who dwellest in heaven.

Behold, as the eyes of servants * look to the bountiful hands of their masters:

And as the eyes of the handmaid look to the bountiful hands of her mistress: * so are our eyes fixed on the Lord, our God, until he have mercy on us.

Have mercy on us, O

mine, miserére nostri; * quia multum repléti sumus despectióne :

Qui multum repléta est ánima nostra : * oppróbrium abundántibus, et despéctio supérbis.

Glória Patri, &c.

Psalmus cxxiii.

Nisi quia Dóminus erat in nobis, dicat nunc Israël : * Nisi quia Dóminus erat in nobis,

Cum exúrgerent hómines in nos, * forte vivos deglutíssent nos :

Cum irascerétur furor eórum in nos, * fórsitan aqua absorbuísset nos.

Torréntem pertransívit ánima nostra : * forsitan pertransísset ánima nostra aquam intollerábilem.

Benedíctus Dóminus,

Lord, have mercy on us : * for we are overwhelmed with humiliation :

For our soul is deeply afflicted : * being an object of reproach to the rich, and of contempt to the proud.

Glory be to the Father, &c.

Psalm 123.

If it had not been that the Lord was with us, let Israel now say : * If it had not been that the Lord was with us,

When men rose up against us, * perhaps they had ingulphed us alive :

When their fury raged against us, * they would have probably overpowered us, like a raging wave, and sunk us.

Our soul has waded across the torrent : * perhaps our soul has passed through waves of the most intolerable evils.

Blessed be the Lord,

* qui non dedit nos in captiónem dentibus eórum.

Anima nostra sicut passer erépta est * de láqueo venántium.

Láqueus contrítus est, * et nos liberáti sumus.

Adjutórium nostrum in nómine Dómini, * qui fecit cœlum et terram.

Glória Patri, &c.

Psalmus cxxiv.

Qui confídunt in Dómino, sicut mons Sion : non commovébitur in æternum, qui hábitat in Jerúsalem.

Montes in circúitu ejus : * et Dóminus in circúita pópuli sui, ex hoc nunc, et usque in sæculum.

Quia non relinquet Dóminus virgam peccatórem super sortem justórum : * ut non exten-

* who has not delivered us a prey to be torn by their teeth.

Our soul has been saved, * like a sparrow, which escapes the snare of the fowlers.

The snare has been broken, * and we are delivered.

Our help is in the name of the Lord, * who made heaven and earth.

Glory be to the Father, &c.

Psalm 124.

They, who trust in the Lord, shall be as Mount Sion : * he, who dwelleth in Jerusalem, shall never be disturbed.

Mountains encompass it on every side : * the Lord doth protect his people, now, and for evermore.

Because the Lord will not permit the chastisement of sinners to fall on the righteous : * lest

dant justi ad iniquitátem manus suas.

Bénefac, Dómine, bonis * et rectis corde.

Declinántes autem in obligationes, addúcet Dóminus cum operántibus iniquitátem : * pax super Israël.

Glória Patri, &c.

(*Per annum*) *Antiphona*. In odórum unguentórum tuórum cúrrimus, adolescéntulæ dilexérunt te nimis.

(*In Adventu*) *Antiphona*. Ne tímeas María, invenísti grátiam apud Dóminum : ecce concípies, et páries fílium.

(*Tempore Nativ.*) *Antiphona*. Rubum, quem víderat Móyses incombústum, conservátam agnóvimus tuam laudábilem virginitátem : Dei

the just be induced to stain their hands with iniquity.

Be kind, O Lord, to those, who are good, * and to the upright of heart.

But such as are inclined to deceive and to ensnare, the Lord shall number among the workers of iniquity : * peace upon Israel.

Glory be to the Father, &c.

(*Through the year*) *Anthem*. We run after the odour of thy perfumes : the young virgins have exceedingly loved thee.

(*In Advent*) *Anthem*. Fear not, Mary, thou hast found grace with the Lord : behold, thou shalt conceive, and bring forth a son.

(*Christmas time*) *Anthem*. In the bush which Moyses saw burn without consuming, we acknowledge the preservation of thy admirable

génitrix intercéde pro nobis.

virginity : O Mother of God, make intercession for us.

(Little Chapter through the year, except in Advent.)

Capitulum. Eccli. xxiv.

Et radicávi in pópuló honorificáto, et in parte Dei mei hæréditas illíus, et in plenitúdine sanctórum deténtio mea. *R.* Deo grátias.

Little Chapter. Ec. 24.

I settled myself among a people, whom the Lord hath honoured, and hath chosen for his portion and inheritance, and I have fixed my abode in the company of all the saints. *R.* Thanks be to God.

(In Advent.)

Capitulum. Lucæ i.

Dabit illi Dóminus Deus sedem David patris ejus, et regnábit in domo Jacob in ætérnum, et regni ejus non erit finis. *R.* Deo grátias.

Little Chapter. Luke 1.

The Lord God will give him the throne of his Father David, and he will eternally reign over the house of Jacob, and his kingdom shall never end. *R.* Thanks be to God.

V. Benedícta tu in muliéribus. *R.* Et benedíctus fructus ventris tui.

V. Blessed art thou among women. *R.* And blessed is the fruit of thy womb.

Kyrie eléison. Christe

Lord, have mercy on

eleíson. Kyrie eleíson.

V. Dómine, exáudi oratiónem meam. *R.* Et clamor meus ad te véniat.

Orémus.

(*Per annum*) Concede miséricors Deus, fragilitáti nostræ præsídium; ut qui sanctæ Dei genetrícis memóriam ágimus, intercessiónis ejus auxílio, à nostris iniquitátibus resurgámus. Per eúndem Dóminum nostrum, Jesum Christum, Fílium tuum, qui tecum vivit et regnat in unitáte Spíritus Sancti, Deus, per omnia sæcula sæculórem. *R.* Amen.

(*In Adventu*) Deus, qui de beátæ Maríæ vírginis útero verbum tuum, Angelo nunciánte, carnem suscípere voluísti; præsta supplícibus tuis, ut qui veré, eam genitrícem Dei crédimus, ejus apud te intercess-

us. Christ, have mercy on us. Lord, have mercy on us.

V. O Lord, hear my prayer. *R.* And let my cry come unto thee.

Let us pray.

(*Through the year*) Grant us, O merciful God, strength against all our weakness; that we, who celebrate the memory of the holy mother of God, may by the help of her intercession rise again from our iniquities. Through the same Lord, Jesus Christ, thy Son, who liveth and reigneth with thee and the Holy Ghost, one God, world without end. *R.* Amen.

(*In Advent*) O God, who wast pleased that thy eternal word, when the angel delivered his message, should take flesh in the womb of the blessed Virgin Mary, give ear to our humble petitions, and grant, that

siónibus adjuvemur.—
Per eundem Dóminum
nostrum, Jesum Christum, Fílium tuum, qui
tecum vivit et regnat,
&c.

(*Tempore Nativ.*)
Deus, qui salútis ætérnæ, beátæ Maríæ virginitáti fœcúnda, humáno géneri præmia præstitísti: tríbue, quæsumus, ut ipsam pro nobis intercédere sentiámus, per quam merúimus auctórem vitæ suscípere, Dóminum nostrum, Jesum Christum, Fílium tuum: Qui tecum vivit et regnat in unitáte Spíritus Sancti, Deus, per ómnia sæcula sæculórum. *R.* Amen.

V. Dómine, exáudi oratiónem meam. *R.* Et clamor meus ad te véniat.

V. Benedicámus Dómino. *R.* Deo grátias.

V. Fidélium ánimæ,

we, who believe her to be truly the Mother of God, may be helped by her prayers. Through the same Lord, Jesus Christ, thy Son, who liveth and reigneth with thee, &c.

(*Christmas time.*) O God, who, by the fruitful virginity of blessed Mary, hast given to mankind the rewards of eternal salvation: grant, we beseech thee, that we may experience her intercession for us, by whom we deserved to receive the Author of life, our Lord, Jesus Christ, thy Son, who liveth and reigneth with thee and the Holy Ghost, one God, world without end. *R.* Amen.

V. O Lord, hear my prayer. *R.* And let my cry come unto thee.

V. Let us bless the Lord. *R.* Thanks be to God.

V. May the souls of

per misericórdiam Dei, requiéscant in pace. *R.* Amen.

the faithful departed, through the mercy of God, rest in peace. *R.* Amen.

AT NONE.

O DIVINE and adorable Lord, Jesus Christ, who hast graciously redeemed us by thy bitter passion and death; we offer up this hour of None to thy honour and glory, and most humbly beseech thee, through the torments and agony thou didst suffer when hanging for three hours on the cross, and through thy precious death, which gave redemption and life to the world, and thy sacred burial, to grant us thy divine assistance, and the grace of the holy sacraments at our last hour and agony, and to give us a happy death, precious in thy sight, and pure from the least defilement of sin, that we may be at our death attended by thy holy angels, and by them borne up on high into those blissful regions, where we will contemplate thy divinity for evermore. Amen.

Ave, María, &c.

V. DEUS in adjutórium meum inténde. *R.* Dómine ad adjuvandum, me festína.

Glória Patri, &c.

Hail, Mary, &c.

V. INCLINE unto my aid, O God. *R.* O Lord, make haste to help me.

Glory be to the Father, &c.

Hymnus.

MEMENTO, rerum, &c.

(*Per annum*) *Antiphona.* Pulchra es, et decóra.

(*In Adventu*) *Antiphona.* Ecce ancílla Dómini.

Hymn.

REMEMBER thou, &c.

(*Through the year*) *Anthem.* Thou art fair and beautiful.

(*In Advent*) *Anthem.* Behold the handmaid of the Lord.

(*Tempore Nativ.*) *Antiphona.* Ecce María génuit.

Psalmus cxxv.

In converténdo Dóminus captivitátem Sion, * facti sumus sicut consolati.

Tunc replétum est gáudio os nostrum : * et lingua nostri exultatióne.

Tunc dicent inter Gentes : * Magnificávit Donus fácere cum eis.

Magnificávit Dóminus fácere nobíscum : * facti sumus lætántes.

Convértere, Dómine, captivitátem nostram,* sicut torrens in Austro.

Qui séminat in lácrymis, * in exultatióne metent.

Eúntes ibant et flebant, * mittentes sémina sua.

Veniéntes autem vé-

(*Christmas time*) *Anthem.* Behold, Mary hath borne.

Psalm 125.

When the Lord brings back the captives of Sion, * we shall be like men cheered with comfort.

Then shall our voices break forth in joyful praises:* and our tongue in canticles of jubilee.

Then shall they declare to their neighbours : * That the Lord hath done great things for them.

The Lord hath done great things for us: * we are therefore become joyful.

Bring back, O Lord, our captive people, * like a torrent in the south.

They, who sow in tears, * shall reap in joy.

They went forth shedding tears, * while they were sowing the seeds.

But they will return

nient cum exultatióne, * portántes manípulos suos.

Glória Patri, &c.

Psalmus cxxvi.

Nisi Dóminus ædificáverit domum, * in vanum laboravérunt, qui ædíficant eam.

Nisi Dóminus custodíerit civitátem, frustra vígilat, qui custódit eam.

Vanum est vobis ante lucem súrgere : * súrgite postquam sedéritis, qui manducátis panem dolóris.

Cum déderit diléctis suis somnum : * ecce, hæreditas Dómini, fílii, merces fructus ventris.

Sicut sagíttæ in manu poténtis, * ita fílii excussórum.

Beátus vir, qui implé-

full of joy, * bringing in the sheaves they have gathered.

Glory be to the Father, &c.

Psalm 126.

Unless the Lord himself shall build up the house, they toil in vain, who strive to build it,

Unless the Lord shall guard the city, * the sentinel doth watch in vain.

It is useless for you to rise before the light ; * arise after you have taken rest, you who eat the bread of sorrow.

Since he will give sleep to his beloved ones ; * know that children are blessings from the Lord, and that a numerous offspring is also a reward.

Like arrows in the hand of a powerful man, * are the children of those who have been reproved.

Blessed is the man,

vit desidérium suum ex ipsis ; * non confundétur, cum loquétur inimícis suis in porta.

Glória Patri, &c.

Psalmus cxxvii.

Beati omnes, qui timent Dóminum, * qui ámbulant in viis ejus.

Labóres mánuum tuárum quia manducábis : * beátus es, et bene tibi erit.

Uxor tua sicut vitis abúndans, * in latéribus domus tuæ.

Fílii tui, sicut novéllæ olivárum, * in circúitu mensæ tuæ.

Ecce, sic benedicétur homo, * qui timet Dóminum.

Benedícat tibi Dóminus ex Sion ; * et videas bona Jerúsalem ómni-

whose desires are accomplished in them ; * he shall not be confounded, when he shall speak to his enemies before the courts.

Glory be to the Father, &c.

Psalm 127.

Blessed are all, who fear the Lord, * who walk according to his ways.

Because thou shalt partake of the labour of thy own hands : * thou art happy, and replenished with all good things.

Thy wife shall be like a fruitful vine, * in a garden at the rere of thy house.

Thy children, like young olive plants, * all round thy table.

Behold, thus shall the man be blessed, * who feareth the Lord.

May the Lord bless thee from Sion ; * and mayest thou see the

bus diébus vitæ tuæ.

Et videas fílios filiórum tuórum, * pacem super Israël.

Glória Patri, &c.

(*Per annum*) *Antiphona.* Pulchra es et decóra, fília Jerúsalem, terríbilis ut castrórum ácies ordináta.

(*In Adventu*) *Antiphona.* Ecce ancílla Dómini : fiat mihi secúndùm verbum tuum.

(*Tempore Nativ.*) *Antiphona.* Ecce, María génuit nobis Salvatórem, quem Joánnes videns, exclamávit, dicens : Ecce Agnus Dei, ecce qui tollit peccáta mundi, alleluia.

prosperity of Jerusalem all the days of thy life.

And mayest thou see the sons of thy children, * and peace given to Israel.

Glory be to the Father, &c.

(*Through the year*) *Anthem.* Thou art fair and beautiful, O daughter of Jerusalem, formidable as an army in battle array.

(*In Advent*) *Anthem.* Behold the handmaid of the Lord : be it done unto me according to thy word.

(*Christmas time*) *Anthem.* Behold, Mary hath borne to us the Saviour, whom John seeing, exclaimed : Behold the Lamb of God, behold him, who taketh away the sins of the world, alleluia.

(*The Little Chapter through the year, except in Advent.*)

Capitulum. Eccli. xxiv.   *Little Chapter. Ec.* 24.

In platéis sicut cinna-   I yielded forth a fra-

mómum et bálsamum aromatízans odórem dedi: quasi myrrha elécta dedi suavitátem odóris. R. Deo grátias.

grant perfume in the streets, like cinnamon and aromatic balm: and, like the best myrrh, I spread around the sweetest odour. R. Thanks be to God.

(*In Advent.*)

Capitulum. Isaiæ vii.

Ecce virgo concípiet, et páriet fílium, et vocábitur nomen ejus Emmánuel. Butyrum et mel cómedet, ut sciat reprobáre malum, et elígere bonum. R. Deo grátias.

Little Chapter. Isa. 7.

Behold, a Virgin shall conceive, and bring forth a son, and his name shall be called Emmanuel. He shall eat butter and honey, that he may know how to reject evil, and choose good. R. Thanks be to God.

V. Post partum Virgo inviolata permansísti. R. Dei génitrix, intercéde pro nobis.

V. After child-birth thou didst remain a pure virgin. R. O Mother of God, intercede for us.

Kyrie eleíson. Christe eleíson. Kyrie eleíson.

Lord, have mercy on us. Christ, have mercy on us. Lord, have mercy on us.

V. Dómine, exáudi oratiónem meam. R. Et clamor meus ad te véniat.

V. O Lord, hear my prayer. R. And let my cry come unto thee.

NONE. 137

Oremus.

(*Per annum.*) Famulorum tuórum, quæsumus, Dómine, delíctis ignósce : ut qui tibi placére de áctibus nostris non valémus, genitrícis Fílii tui Dómini nostri intercessióne salvémur : Qui tecum vivit et regnat, in unitáte Spíritus Sancti, Deus, per ómnia sæcula sæculórum. *R.* Amen.

Let us pray.

(*Through the year*) Pardon, we beseech thee, O Lord, the sins of thy servants : that we, who are not able to please thee by our own actions, may be saved by the intercession of the Mother of thy Son, our Lord : Who liveth and reigneth with thee, and the Holy Ghost, one God, world without end. *R.* Amen.

(*In Advent.*)

(*In Adventu.*) Deus, qui de beátæ Maríæ vírginis útero, Verbum tuum, Angelo nuntiánte, carnem suscípere voluísti : præsta supplícibus tuis ; ut qui verè eam genitrícem Dei crédimus, ejus apud te intercessiónibus adjuvémur. Per eúmdem Dóminum nostrum, Jesum Christum, Fílium tuum, qui tecum vivit et regnat in unitàte Spíritus Sancti, Deus, per ómnia sæcula

(*In Advent*) O God, who wast pleased that thy eternal Word, when the angel delivered his message, should take flesh in the womb of the blessed Virgin Mary : give ear to our humble petitions, and grant that we, who believe her to be truly the Mother of God, may be helped by her prayers. Through the same Lord, Jesus Christ, thy Son, who liveth and reigneth

sæculórum. *R.* Amen.

(*Tempore Nativ.*) Deus, qui salútis ætérnæ, beátæ Maríæ virginitáte fœcúnda, humáno géneri præmia præstitísti; tríbue, quæsumus, ut ipsam pro nobis intercédere sentiámus, per quam merúimus auctórem vitæ suscípere, Dóminum nostrum, Jesum Christum, Fílium tuum: Qui tecum vivit et regnat, &c.

V. Dómine, exáudi oratiónem meam. *R.* Et clamor meus ad te véniat.

V. Benedicámus Dómino. *R.* Deo grátias.

V. Fidélium ánimæ, per misericórdiam Dei, requiéscant in pace. *R.* Amen.

Pater noster, &c. *Secreto.*

thee, and the Holy Ghost, one God, world without end. *R.* Amen.

(*Christmas time*) O God, who by the fruitful virginity of blessed Mary, hast given to mankind the rewards of eternal salvation; grant, we beseech thee, that we may experience her intercession for us, by whom we have received the author of life, our Lord, Jesus, Christ, thy Son, who liveth and reigneth with thee, &c.

V. O Lord, hear my prayer. *R.* And let my cry come unto thee.

V. Let us bless the Lord. *R.* Thanks be to God.

V. May the souls of the faithful departed, through the mercy of God, rest in peace. *R.* Amen.

Our Father, &c. *In silence.*

The Prayer after Office, and thus the lesser Hours are terminated.

When the Office is said in Choir, after the Lord's Prayer is said the following Versicle:—

V. Dóminus det nobis suam pacem. R. Et vitam ætérnam. Amen.

V. May the Lord grant us his peace. R. And eternal life. Amen.

Then one of the Anthems of the Blessed Virgin Mary, according to the time of the year, as before, at the end of Complin.

V. Divínum auxílium máneat semper nobíscum. R. Amen.

V. May the divine assistance always remain with us. R. Amen.

The Prayer after Office, May all praise, honour, &c. *as before.*

END OF THE OFFICE OF THE B. V. M.

GRACES BEFORE AND AFTER MEALS.

Before Dinner.

Superior. Benedícite.

The rest answer. Benedícite.

V. Oculi ómnium.

R. In te sperant Domine, et tu das escam illórum in tempore opportúno. Aperis tu manum tuam, et imples omne ánimal benedictione.

Gloria Patri, &c.

Sicut erat, &c.

Kyrie eleíson. Christe eleison. Kyrie eleíson.

Pater noster, (*in secreto.*)

V. Et ne nos inducas in tentatiónem.

R. Sed líbera nos à malo.

Oremus.

Benedic Domine nos, et tua dona, quæ

Sup. Let us give thanks.

R. Let us thank God.

V. The eyes of all,

R. Hope in thee, O Lord, and thou givest them food in due season. Thou openest thine hand, and fillest every living creature by thy bounty.

Glory be to the Father, &c.

As it was in the beginning, &c.

Lord have mercy on us. Christ have mercy on us. Lord have mercy on us.

Our Father (*in secret*).

V. And lead us not into temptation.

R. But deliver us from evil.

Let us pray.

Bless us, O Lord, and these thy gifts, of which,

GRACES BEFORE AND AFTER MEALS.

de tua largitáte sumus sumptúri. Per Christum Dominum nostrum. *R.* Amen.

Reader. Jube Domine benedícere.

Benediction. Mensæ cælestis participes fáciat nos Rex æternæ glóriæ. *R.* Amen.

of thy bounty, we are now going to partake. Thro' Christ, our Lord. *R.* Amen.

Reader. Command us, O Lord, to give thee thanks.

Benediction. May the King of eternal glory grant that we be partakers of the heavenly banquet. *R.* Amen.

After Dinner.

Reader. Tu autem Domine miserére nobis.

R. Deo gratias.

Superior. V. Confiteántur tibi Domine ómnia opera tua. *R.* Et Sancti tui benedícant tibi.

V. Gloria Patri, &c.

R. Sicut erat, &c.

Superior. Agimus tibi grátias omnipotens Deus, pro universis benefíciis tuis: qui vivis et regnas in sæcula sæculórum. R. Amen.

Reader. But do thou, O Lord, have mercy upon us.

R. Let us give thanks unto God.

Sup. V. Let all thy works, O Lord, confess unto thee. *R.* And let thy saints bless thee.

V. Glory be to the Father, &c.

R. As it was in the beginning, &c.

Sup. We give thee thanks, O Almighty God, for all thy kindnesses; who livest and reignest for ever and ever. *R.* Amen.

Psalmus cxvi.

Laudate Dominum omnes gentes: * laudáte eum omnes populi.

Quóniam confirmáta est super nos misericórdia ejus: * et veritas Domini manet in æternum.

Gloria Patri, &c.

Sicut erat, &c.

Kyrie eleíson. Christe eleíson. Kyrie eleíson.

Pater noster, &c.

V. Et ne nos indúcas in tentatiónem.

R. Sed libera nos a malo.

V. Dispérsit, dedit pauperibus.

R. Justítia ejus manet in sæculum sæculi.

V. Benedícam Dominum in omni tempore.

R. Semper laus ejus in ore meo.

V. In Domino laudábitur anima mea.

R. Audiánt mansuéti, et lætentur.

Psalm 116.

Praise the Lord, all ye nations : * praise him, all ye people.

Because his mercy is established over us: * and his truth endureth for ever.

Glory be to the Father, &c.

As it was, &c.

Lord have mercy upon us. Christ have mercy upon us. Lord have mercy upon us.

Our Father, &c.

V. And lead us not into temptation.

R. But deliver us from evil.

V. He distributed and gave unto the poor.

R. His justice abideth for ever and ever.

V. I shall bless the Lord at all times.

R. His praise shall be always in my mouth.

V. In the Lord shall my soul be praised.

R. Let the meek hear and be glad.

V. Magnificate Dominum mecum.

R. Et exultémus nomen ejus in idípsum.

V. Sit nomen Domini benedíctum.

R. Ex hoc nunc et usque in sæculum.

Retribúere dignáre Domine ómnibus nobis bona facientibus propter nomen tuum vitam æternum. *R.* Amen.

V. Benedicámus Domino.

R. Deo grátias. *V.* Fidelium ánimæ per misericórdiam Dei requiescant in pace. *R.* Amen.

Pater noster, &c. *in secreto.*

Deus det nobis suam pacem. *R.* Amen.

Psalmus l.

Miserere mei, Deus, * secundum magnam misericordiam tuam.

Et secundum multitudinem miserationum tuarum, * dele iniquitatem meam.

V. Magnify the Lord with me.

R. And let us exalt his name.

V. Blessed be the name of the Lord.

R. Now and evermore.

Vouchsafe, O Lord, to grant eternal life unto us all who act righteously, for thy name's sake. *R.* Amen.

V. Let us bless the Lord.

R. Let us give thanks unto God. *V.* May the souls of the faithful, through the mercy of God, rest in peace. *R.* Amen.

Our Father, &c. *in secret.*

O God, grant us thy peace. *R.* Amen.

Psalm 50.

Have mercy on me, O God, * according to thy great mercy.

And according to the multitude of thy tender mercies, * blot out my iniquities.

Amplius lava mea ab iniquitate mea : * et a peccato meo munda me.

Quoniam iniquitatem meam ego cognosco : * et peccatum meum contra me est semper.

Tibi soli peccavi, et malum coram te feci : * ut justificeris in sermonibus tuis, et vincas cum judicaris.

Ecce enim iniquitatibus conceptus sum : * et in pecattis concepit me mater mea.

Ecce enim veritatem dilexisti : incerta et occulta sapientiæ tuæ manifestasti mihi.

Asperges me hyssopo, et mundabor : * lavabis me, et super nivem dealbabor.

Auditui meo dabis gaudium et lætitiam : *

Wash me yet more from my iniquity : * and cleanse me from my sin.

For I know my iniquity : and my sin is always against me.

To thee alone have I sinned, and have done evil in thy presence : * I acknowledge it, that thou mayest be justified in thy judgment, and mayest prevail in thy just sentence.

Behold, I was conceived in iniquities : * and in sins did my mother conceive me.

Thou hast loved truth, * and hast revealed to me the mysterious and hidden secrets of thy divine wisdom.

Thou wilt sprinkle me with hyssop, and I shall be cleansed ; * thou wilt wash me, and I shall be made whiter than snow.

Thou wilt speak to me words of consolation and

et exultabunt ossa humiliata.

Averte faciem tuam a peccatis meis : * et omnes iniquitates meas dele.

Cor mundum crea in me, Deus : * et spiritum rectum innova in visceribus meis.

Ne projicias me a facie tua : * et spiritum sanctum tuum ne auferas a me.

Redde mihi lætitiam salutaris tui ; * et spiritu principali confirma me.

Docebo iniquos vias tuas : * et impii ad te convertentur.

Libera me de sanguinibus, Deus, Deus salutis meæ : et exultabit lingua mea justitiam tuam.

Domine, labia mea aperies : * et os meum

of joy ; * and this wretched being of mine shall rejoice.

Turn away thy thoughts from my sins ; * and cancel all my iniquities.

Render my heart pure and clean, O God, * and renew within me a spirit of righteousness.

Cast me not away from thy presence ; * and take not thy holy Spirit from me.

Impart unto me the joy of thy salutary graces : * and strengthen me with the spirit of true piety.

I will teach the unjust thy ways : * and the wicked shall be converted to thee.

Deliver me from my crimes of blood, O great God, my Saviour ; * and my tongue shall joyfully proclaim thy justice.

O Lord, thou wilt open my lips, * and my

annuntiabit laudem tuam.

Quoniam si voluisses sacrificium dedissem utique : * holocaustis non delectaberis.

Sacrificium Deo spiritus contribulatus : * cor contritum et humiliatum, Deus, non despicies.

Benigne fac, Domine, in bona voluntate tua Sion : * ut ædificentur muri Jerusalem.

Tunc acceptabis sacrificium justitiæ, oblationes, et holocausta : * tunc imponent super altare tuum vitulos.

Glória Patri, &c.

Oremus.

Respice, quæsumus Domine, super hanc famíliam tuam, pro qua

tongue shall declare thy praise.

For if thou hadst desired a sacrifice, I would indeed have offered it up to thee : * with whole-burnt offerings thou wilt not be well pleased.

The sacrifice, which God requires, is a repentant spirit : * a contrite and humble heart, O God, thou wilt not despise.

Shew thy kind will, O Lord, to Sion : * that the walls of Jerusalem may be built up.

Then wilt thou accept the sacrifices of righteousness, of oblations, and of whole-burnt offerings : * then shall they immolate victims on thy altars.

Glory be to the Father, &c.

Let us pray.

Look down, O Lord, we beseech thee, upon this thy family, for

Dominus noster Jesus Christus non dubitávit mánibus tradi nocentium. Pater noster, *in secret*.

whom our Lord Jesus Christ freely suffered himself to be delivered into the hands of sinners. Our Father, &c. *in secret*.

BEFORE SUPPER.

Superior. Benedicite.

The rest answer. Benedicite.

Superior. Edent páuperes, et saturabúntur, et laudábunt Dominum, qui requírunt eum: vivent corda eorum in sæculum sæculi.

Glória Patri, &c.

Sicut erat, &c. Kyrie eleison. Christe eleison. Kyrie eleison.

Pater noster, *in secret*.

V. Et ne nos inducas in tentatiónem.

R. Sed libera nos a malo.

Superior. Bless the Lord.

Answer. Give thanks unto the Lord.

Superior. The poor shall eat and be filled; and they who seek the Lord will praise him: their hearts shall live for evermore.

Glory be to the Father, &c.

As it was in the beginning, &c. Lord have mercy upon us. Christ have mercy upon us. Lord have mercy upon us.

Our Father, &c. *in secret*.

V. And lead us not into temptation.

R. But deliver us from evil.

GRACES BEFORE AND AFTER MEALS.

Oremus.	Let us pray.

BENEDIC Domine nos, et hæc tua dona, quæ de tua largitáte sumus sumptúri. Per Christum Dominum nostrum. *R.* Amen.

POUR, O Lord, thy blessing upon us, and upon those thy gifts, which of thy great bounty we are about to partake of. Through Jesus Christ our Lord. *R.* Amen.

Reader. Jube Domine benedícere.

Reader. Command us, O Lord, to give thee thanks.

Superior. Ad cænam vitæ æternæ perdúcat nos Rex æternæ gloriæ. *R.* Amen.

Superior. May the King of eternal Glory bring us into life everlasting. *R.* Amen.

AFTER SUPPER.

Psalmus cxvi.

Psalm 116.

Laudate Dominum, &c.

Praise ye the Lord, &c.

Canticum beatæ Mariæ Virginis. Lucæ i. xlvi.

Canticle of the blessed Virgin Mary. Luke 1. 46.

Magnificat * anima mea Dominum.

My soul doth magnify * the Lord.

Et exultavit spiritus meus * in Deo salutari meo.

And my spirit hath rejoiced * in God my Saviour.

Quia respexit humilitatem ancillæ suæ : * ecce enim ex hoc bea-

Because he hath regarded the humility of his handmaid : * behold

tam me dicent omnes generationes.	from henceforth all generations shall call me blessed.
Quia fecit mihi magna, qui potens es; * sanctum nomen ejus.	For he who is mighty, hath done great things to me: * and holy is his name.
Et misericordia ejus a progenie in progenies * timentibus eum.	And his mercy is from generation to generation * to those who fear him.
Fecit potentiam in brachio suo : * dispersit superbos mente cordis sui.	He hath shewn might in his arm : * he hath scattered the proud in the conceit of their heart.
Deposuit potentes de sede, * et exaltavit humiles.	He hath cast down the mighty from their seat, * and hath exalted the humble.
Esurientes implevit bonis, * et divites dimisit inanes.	He hath filled the hungry with good things, * and the rich he hath sent away empty.
Suscepit Israel puerum suum * recordatus misericordiæ suæ.	He hath received Israel, his servant, * being mindful of his mercy.
Sicut locutus est ad patres nostros ; * Abraham, et semini ejus in sæcula.	As he spoke to our Fathers ; * to Abraham and to his seed for ever.
Gloria Patri, &c.	Glory be to the Father, &c.

V. Ora pro nobis sancta Dei genetrix.

R. Ut digni efficiámur promissionibus Christi.

Oremus.

Concede miséricors Deus fragilitáti nostræ præsidium: ut qui sanctæ Dei genitricis memóriam ágimus, intercessionibus ejus auxílio a nostris iniquitatibus resurgamus. Per eumdem Christum Dominum nostrum. *R.* Amen.

V. Pray for us, O holy Mother of God.

R. That we may be made worthy of the promises of Christ.

Let us pray.

O merciful God, grant thy protection unto our frail and erring nature, that we, who commemorate the holy Mother of God, may, by the assistance of her intercession, be rescued from our iniquities.— Thro' the same Christ our Lord. *R.* Amen.

The foregoing manner of giving Grace before and after Meals is observed throughout the year, except on the following days, when the V. is only changed:—

ON CHRISTMAS DAY,

And until the Supper of the Vigil of the Epiphany exclusively.

BEFORE DINNER.

V. Verbum caro factum est, alleluia.

R. Et habitavit in nobis, alleluia.

Gloria Patri, &c.

Sicut erat, &c.

V. The word was made flesh, alleluia.

R. And dwelt amongst us, alleluia.

Glory be to the Father, &c.

As it was in the beginning, &c.

AFTER DINNER.

V. Notum fecit Dominus, alleluia.

R. Salutare suum, alleluia.

The rest as before.

V. The Lord hath made known, alleluia.

R. His salvation, alleluia.

The rest as before.

ON THE EPIPHANY,
AND DURING THE OCTAVE.

BEFORE DINNER.

V. Reges Tharsis, et insulæ munera offerent, alleluia.

R. Reges Arabum et Saba dona adducent, alleluia.

Gloria Patri, &c.

Sicut erat, &c.

V. The Kings of Tharsis and the islands shall offer thee presents, alleluia.

R. The Kings of the Arabians and Saba shall bring gifts unto thee, alleluia.

Glory be to the Father, &c.

As it was in the beginning, &c.

AFTER DINNER.

V. Omnes de Saba venient, alleluia.

R. Aurum et thus deferéntes, alleluia.

Gloria Patri, &c.

Sicut erat, &c.

V. All the people of Saba shall come, alleluia.

R. Bringing forth their gold and incense, alleluia.

Glory be to the Father, &c.

As it was in the beginning, &c.

ON HOLY THURSDAY.

BEFORE DINNER.

V. Christus factus est pro nobis obédiens usque ad mortem. Pater noster, &c. *all in secret.*

V. Christ became for our sakes obedient even unto death. Our Father, &c. *in secret.*

AFTER DINNER.

V. Christus factus est pro nobis obédiens usque ad mortem.

V. Christ became for our sakes obedient even unto death.

Psalmus l.

Psalm 50.

Gloria Patri, *is not said.*

Glory be to the Father, *is not said.*

Pater noster, &c. *in secret.*

Our Father, &c. *in secret.*

Oremus.

Let us pray.

Respice, quæsumus Domine, super hanc famíliam tuam, pro qua Dominus noster Jesus Christus non dubitavit manibus tradi nocentium, et crucis subíre tormentum.

Look down, we beseech thee, O Lord, upon this thy family, for whom our Lord Jesus Christ freely suffered himself to be delivered into the hands of sinners, and to undergo the torments of the Cross.

Pater noster, *in secret.*

Our Father, *in secret.*

Fidélium animæ, &c. *nor* Deus det nobis suam pacis, *is not said here.*

May the souls of the faithful, &c., *nor* May God grant us his peace, *is not said here.*

ON GOOD FRIDAY.
BEFORE DINNER.

V. Christus factus est pro nobis obédiens usque ad mortem, mortem autem Crucis.

V. Christ became for our sakes obedient unto death, even the death of the Cross.

The rest as on the preceding day.

ON HOLY SATURDAY.
BEFORE DINNER.

V. Benedicite. *R.* Benedicite.

V. Give benediction. *R.* Bless ye the Lord.

V. Vespere autem sabbati, quæ lucescit in prima sabbati, alleluia.

V. But in the evening which shineth in the first Sabbath, alleluia.

R. Venit Maria Magdalene, et áltera Maria videre sepúlchrum, alleluia.

R. Mary Magdalene and the other Mary, came to see the sepulchre, alleluia.

Gloria Patri, &c.

Glory be to the Father, &c.

Sicut erat, &c.

As it was in the beginning, &c.

AFTER DINNER.

V. Vespere autem, &c. *as above.*

V. But in the evening, &c. *as above.*

Gloria Patri, &c.

Glory be to the Father, &c.

Psalmus cxvi.

Psalm 116.

Laudate Dominum omnes gentes : * laudate eum omnes populi.

Praise the Lord, all ye nations : * praise him all ye people.

Quóniam confirmata est super nos misericórdia ejus: * et veritas Domini manet in aeternum.

Because his mercy is established upon us: * and the truth of the Lord abideth for ever.

Gloria Patri, &c.

Glory be to the Father, &c.

ON EASTER SUNDAY,

And until the Supper of the following Saturday, exclusively.

BEFORE DINNER.

V. Hæc dies quam fecit Dominus, alleluia.

V. This day which the Lord hath made, alleluia.

R. Exultémus et lætemur in ea, alleluia.

R. Let us dance with joy, and rejoice in it, alleluia.

Gloria Patri, &c.

Glory be to the Father, &c.

AFTER DINNER.

V. Hæc dies, &c. *as above.*

V. This day, &c. *as above.*

ON ASCENSION THURSDAY,

And until the Supper of the Vigil of Pentecost, exclusively.

BEFORE DINNER.

V. Ascendet Deus in jubilatióne, alleluia.

V. God will ascend in jubilee, alleluia.

Gloria Patri, &c.

Glory be to the Father, &c.

AFTER DINNER.

V. Ascéndens Christus in altum, alleluia.
R. Captívam duxit capturtátem, alleluia.
Gloria Patri, &c.

V. Christ ascending on high, alleluia.
R. Led captivity captive, alleluia.
Glory be to the Father, &c.

FROM THE VIGIL OF PENTECOST,

Inclusively, until the Supper of the Saturday following, exclusively.

BEFORE DINNER.

V. Spiritus Domini replevit orbem terrárum, alleluia.
R. Et hoc quod continet omnia scientiam habet vocis, alleluia.
Gloria Patri, &c.

V. The spirit of the Lord hath filled the earth, alleluia.
R. And that which contains all knowledge, let us praise, alleluia.
Glory be to the Father, &c.

AFTER DINNER.

V. Repléti sunt spíritu sancto, alleluia.
R. Et coepérunt loqui, alleluia.

V. They were filled with the Holy Ghost, alleluia.
R. And began to speak, alleluia.

☞ The Supper Grace is said at Dinner on Fast Days, on which the Vespers are said before Dinner.

CATHOLIC WORKS,

TO BE HAD OF
RICHARD GRACE AND SON.

I.
THE DUTIES AND SANCTITY OF THE RELIGIOUS STATE.
From the French of De Rance, 2 vols.

II.
LIFE OF ST. JANE FRANCES DE CHANTEL,
Foundress and first Superior of the Order of THE VISITATION.

III.
THE SINNER'S CONVERSION
Reduced to principle.

IV.
THE SCHOOL OF CHRIST,
From the French of L'Abbe Grou.

V.
VISITS TO THE BLESSED SACRAMENT, and TO THE BLESSED VIRGIN,
For every Day in the Month.

VI.
SPIRITUAL RETREAT FOR RELIGIOUS PERSONS.

VII.
HUBY'S MEDITATIONS ON DIVINE LOVE,
OR A
SPIRITUAL RETREAT ON THE LOVE OF GOD,
As is found displayed in the great Truths and Mysteries of the Catholic Religion.

With every new Religious Work as published.

Made in the USA
Columbia, SC
14 July 2024